Bloomsbury

ERECTED BY CAMDEN LONDON BOROUGH COUNCIL

HERE AND
IN NEIGHBOURING
HOUSES DURING
THE FIRST HALF OF
THE 20th CENTURY
THERE LIVED SEVERAL
MEMBERS OF THE
BLOOMSBURY GROUP
INCLUDING
VIRGINIA WOOLF
CLIVE BELL AND
THE STRACHEYS

Bloomsbury

Beyond the Establishment

Matthew Ingleby

First published in 2017 by
The British Library
96 Euston Road
London NW1 2DB

British Library Cataloguing in Publication Data
A catalogue record for this book is available from the British Library

ISBN: 978 0 7123 5656 5

Frontispiece: Plaque commemorating the Bloomsbury Group, 50 Gordon
Square, Bloomsbury

Typeset by IDSUK (DataConnection) Ltd
Cover by Sandra Friesen Design
Picture research by Sally Nicholls
Printed in Italy by Lego S.p.A.

Contents

'Wet Winter Evening and a Book Lover in Bloomsbury.' Woman browsing a bookstall in Sicilian Avenue. Photograph in St John Adcock (ed), *Wonderful London*, 1928.

Introduction

When chatting to people about my research on Bloomsbury over the last ten years, I've often found that they know a fair amount about its inhabitants, writings, institutions and events, but are surprisingly hazy about the whereabouts of the place itself. Such is the influence wielded within the popular consciousness by London's Underground map, Bloomsbury being one of those celebrated London localities which, being untethered to the name of any tube station, can prove peculiarly hard to locate.

Actually, the precise cartographical limits that define where Bloomsbury begins and ends have always been a matter of dispute. For the purposes of the straightforwardness of his dimensions, this book goes along with Edward Walford's view, in 1878, that 'the district now known under the general name of Bloomsbury lies on the north side of Holborn, stretching away as far as the Euston Road, and is bounded to the east and west respectively by Gray's Inn Road and Tottenham Court Road.'[1]

These major roads, which form a fairly equal parallelogram, circumscribe Bloomsbury, each of them acting as boundaries that demarcate the place from other neighbourhoods that also have distinct histories and characters. Between the west and the east of the central core of the city, the neighbourhood was for much of its modern history defined as a kind of social threshold between London's rich and poor. As R. W. Surtees put it, in 1843, Bloomsbury was 'a curious locality, – city people considering it west, while those in the west consider it east.'[2]

After the mid-nineteenth century, when three of London's major railway stations were constructed alongside its northern border, Bloomsbury became a cosmopolitan gateway not only to the North and Scotland but, via cities like Liverpool, Glasgow and Hull, to foreign climes too. Meanwhile at its southern border of New Oxford Street, the city's intellectual hub rubbed up against not only the slums of St Giles, but also the theatreland of Covent Garden. According to Wilkie Collins, in 1883, Bloomsbury was 'alike out of the way of fashion and business; and . . . yet within easy reach of the one and the other'.[3] Bloomsbury's identity – betwixt and between – has always been produced out of its dynamic relation to its neighbours.

Bloomsbury gets its first historical mention in the 1086 Domesday Book. The locality's suggestive name, however, doesn't appear in any records until 1201, when William de Blemond, a Norman landowner, was written serendipitously into the history of an unusually fascinating and influential place via the peculiar agency of etymological genetics.

As part of the land redistribution that attended the beginnings of the Reformation, in the sixteenth century the Crown took possession of lands that in the medieval period had been acquired by the Church. Bloomsbury was thus handed over to Thomas Wriothesley, 1st Earl of Southampton, an inheritance that later trickled (or, rather, flowed) down to the Bedfords, an aristocratic family that still possess substantial holdings in the area.

The more interesting part of Bloomsbury's history starts, however, when these post-Reformation landowners began to develop their land, from the seventeenth century onwards. Bloomsbury's interest for readers today does not lie with the few men lucky enough to have inherited its title deeds, but with the many men and women that, living and working in the area, helped produce and circulate ideas, values and lifestyles that were distinctly beyond established norms. The neighbourhood has been consistently at the vanguard of modernity, not only

View of Bedford Square, April 2017.

culturally but also politically, being involved in the development of new forms of philanthropy in the eighteenth century, secular liberalism in the nineteenth century, and social democracy in the twentieth century. Bloomsbury's cultural legacy continues to this day to sustain the hopes of many for more emancipated, egalitarian futures as yet unrealised.

Bloomsbury may have often been positioned beyond the establishment, but it was always, of course, also a part of the establishment. In the early nineteenth century, Tories such as the MP John Wilson Croker and the novelist Theodore Hook satirically lampooned this Whig-owned part of town, on the edge of the city, as embarrassingly marginal to London's established core – the fashionable Courtland region of St James's and Piccadilly. This marginality became felt, over the course of the nineteenth century, by decreasing rental yields and socio-economic decline.

In that same period, however, Bloomsbury gradually established itself as a different kind of centre within a modernising metropolis, one defined by intellectual endeavour and middle-class professionalism. By the early twentieth century, when both the 'Bloomsbury Group' and T. S. Eliot, as editor at Faber, had become associated with the area, Bloomsbury was known as a base for a kind of literary and artistic establishment, which set itself in opposition to what they perceived as the dominant tyranny within modernity – the mass market.

Bloomsbury's history is characterised, then, by its curious relationship to the establishment, the area having transformed itself from a suburb to the centre of writing and thinking in the Anglophone world. Each of the chapters in this book approaches Bloomsbury from an oblique angle to draw out particular aspects of the place, and to shed new light on its complex history and continuing identity.

The opening chapter, 'Budding', explores how Bloomsbury, built upon green fields as part of an unprecedented speculative

50 Gordon Square, Bloomsbury. During the first half of the twentieth century, this and neighbouring houses formed the heart of the Bloomsbury Group.

construction project, has long nourished the young and youthful. The next chapter, 'Aspiring', shows through its architecture how Bloomsbury's secularism might be seen to bear continuities with the religious idealism that its universities and other institutions have often explicitly disavowed.

The exclusivity of Bloomsbury's most famous cultural and intellectual cliques is suggested, in 'Connecting', to be implicitly related to the more accidental social collisions and alliances that its unusual demographic mixture brought to bear, while 'Railing' makes connections between the iron fencing that has materially worked to police Bloomsbury's open spaces and the various kinds of political dissent to have flourished amidst them. 'Timing' proposes that Bloomsbury's relation with the clock has long been peculiarly conflicted between industrial punctuality and bohemian flexibility, while it also addresses the area's notable engagement not only with the deep past but with the future also. 'Wording', finally, draws attention to the juxtaposition and rivalry in Bloomsbury of diverse professions concerned with the limitation, expansion, codification and manipulation of language.

Choosing to conclude this book about a place with a turn to words is partly intended to underline just how important they are to Bloomsbury, being the very materials that allow for the circulation of the locality's most globally important products – ideas. But ending with a chapter about language also, of course, betrays my own particular subjective bias towards literature, which derives from the academic discipline in which I work. I have chosen to tell some of Bloomsbury's interrelated stories largely through the voices of literary figures that have helped to articulate them, through their fiction, drama and poetry.

Other books about Bloomsbury tell other stories in other ways. As do the streets themselves. Beyond the blue plaques that proliferate continually in this part of town, any walk through this locality will open up questions and begin to unearth aspects of the place I have here neglected. If you get bored of this book, and want to know something more about Bloomsbury from what it offers, I suggest putting it down and going for a wander around its streets and squares instead.

The Brunswick Plane, Brunswick Square. One of the original trees that was planted by the Georgians at the time the square was created, this elegant plane tree has been allowed to grow to its natural shape, with low swooping branches.

Chapter 1 **Budding**

The poet Amy Levy was living in Bloomsbury, at 7 Endsleigh Gardens, when she wrote this poem, 'A London Plane-Tree' (1889). It attends to the presence of nature in the midst of the bustling metropolis.

> GREEN is the plane-tree in the square,
>   The other trees are brown;
> They droop and pine for country air;
>   The plane-tree loves the town.
>
> Here from my garret-pane, I mark
>   The plane-tree bud and blow,
> Shed her recuperative bark,
>   And spread her shade below.
>
> Among her branches, in and out,
>   The city breezes play;
> The dun fog wraps her round about;
>   Above, the smoke curls grey.
>
> Others the country take for choice,
>   And hold the town in scorn;
> But she has listened to the voice
>   On city breezes borne.[1]

Since the pastoral verse of Ancient Greece, poets had celebrated nature, placing it in an organic, rural world, far away from the fashion and commerce of the town. For a writer such as Levy, however – Jewish, feminist, gay – late nineteenth-century Bloomsbury's bohemian, cosmopolitan squares were more 'recuperative' than the 'country air' prized by literary tradition. Like the budding plane trees she witnessed from her 'garret-pane', Levy could feel relatively at home amidst the 'dun fog' and 'city breezes' that played around Bloomsbury's plane trees.

Levy was part of a community of women intellectuals, including Eleanor Marx, the daughter of Karl, who studied and wrote in the reading room of British Museum at the end of the nineteenth century. For these women, Bloomsbury enjoyed a special kind of cultural microclimate, which could nourish as much as stifle. As 'A London Plane-Tree' has it, the urban environment of late nineteenth-century Bloomsbury was not only the inspiration for Levy's poetic voice but also provided the material conditions that made it possible.

Bloomsbury is still a surprisingly green neighbourhood. Its garden squares preserve the natural world within the heart of the city, hosting plane trees that function as eco-systems for a range of other flora and fauna – such as the one in Brunswick Square, thought to be the second oldest in London and designated by Trees for Cities as one of London's '10 Great Trees'. The seasons are more noticeable here than in other parts of central London. Wander around Tavistock Square lawn in the spring time and one has to dodge not only the squirrels but the crocuses. In autumn, red and gold leaves pile up around the pavements. If you look hard enough, you will even spot a sheep pen.

This part of central London is unusually 'green' in another sense too, one that also hovers behind Levy's poem, published as it was when she was just twenty-seven years old. Bloomsbury is defined by beginnings and by youth, in all its vulnerability and beauty. The many universities and colleges here – University College London, Birkbeck, SOAS, RADA – mean that its streets and squares are perpetually packed with young people, who replenish the area each year with new thoughts and sensitivities about the world.

The area's academic identity is a legacy of the nineteenth century, with UCL dating back to 1826. Almost a century before that, however, Bloomsbury has been associated with childhood – Thomas Coram founded the Foundling Hospital, off Guilford Street, in 1739. One of the most prominent charitable organisations of the eighteenth century, and supported by celebrities such as the composer Handel and the artist Hogarth, the Foundling Hospital was an orphanage whose Royal Charter dedicated it to 'the maintenance and education of exposed and deserted young children'. In Handel's *Messiah*, a piece of music whose enormous popularity was partly forged through its heavy association with this fashionable charity, one of the most memorable of the mighty choruses opens with 'For unto us a child in born'. Handel directed highly successful performances of *Messiah* multiple times at the Foundling Hospital to raise money for the foundation, beginning with a concert to mark the presentation of a new organ (built by Henry Bevington) on 1 May 1750. Handel was elected a governor of the hospital on the following day. He bequeathed to the hospital a full score of his greatest oratorio, which is still held today at the Foundling Museum.

Today you can visit the Foundling Museum to learn more about Bloomsbury's historical role in protecting and giving opportunities to the unfortunate young victims of a hypocritical moral code. The Foundling's legacy can be found next door in Coram, a charity based in Bloomsbury that continues to work with disadvantaged children. There is also Coram's Fields, the open space on to the north of Lamb's Conduit Street that famously denies access to adults unaccompanied by a child. Go any evening of the week and the football courts are full of local kids taking advantage of scarce inner-city space for outdoor sports.

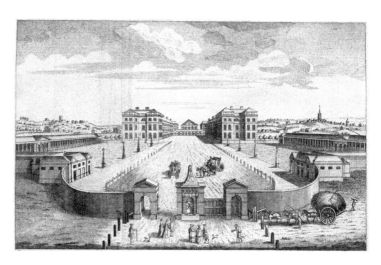

A Perspective View of the Foundling Hospital. Plate dated 1763.

'In the Foundling Hospital Grounds.' Plate from G. R. Sims [ed.], *Living London. Its Work and its Play. Its Humour and its Pathos. Its Sights and its Scenes*, Cassell 1902.

Page from Handel's manuscript for *Messiah*, showing bars from the 'Hallelujah Chorus', 1741

While natural greenness resonates with the area's connection with youth, it reminds us too of its own early years, the area's pre-urban past. Bloomsbury is nowadays in the centre of London, but until the latter part of the eighteenth century it was at the very margins of the city. In the early 1750s, the poet William Cowper frequented 30 Southampton Row daily when he was a legal apprentice. Back then, Southampton Row was at the northern edge of London. One of Cowper's most famous lines insists that 'God made the Country, Man made the Town'. In eighteenth-century Bloomsbury, he had witnessed the blurring of that binary. As he says in his occasional epistolary poem, 'To my dearest cousin on her removal of us from Silver End, to Weston', on walking northwards the cityscape melted into countryside almost immediately:

> Cheerful and happy I was wont to stray
> Through *Ducal Bedford*'s fields to *Primrose Hill.*[2]

Before the 1770s, when master builders such as Thomas Cubitt began to construct a new suburb on the Duke of Bedford's estate, Bloomsbury had been largely made up of fields and gardens, belonging to aristocratic mansions. When the poet Thomas Gray lived in Southampton Row between July 1759 and November 1761, he stressed the neighbourhood's rural feel and the presence of the resident landowners: 'I am now settled in my new territories commanding Bedford gardens, and all the fields as far as Highgate and Hampstead, with such a concourse of moving pictures as would astonish you; so *rus-in-urbe-ish*, that I believe I shall stay here, except little excursions and vagaries, for a year to come . . . here is air, and sunshine, and quiet'.[3]

Less than a decade and half later, in 1775, the construction of Bedford Square would commence London's most aggressive phase of urban sprawl northwards into the countryside. Before long, Bloomsbury was very much part of a modern inner city.

However, its several pockets of green – the squares – would continue to recall its semi-rural past, not only because of their plentiful trees and flowers, but through their names, which conjure aristocratic country houses. 'Woburn Square' reminds us of Woburn Abbey, Bedfordshire (chief seat of the Bedford family); 'Tavistock Square' gestures to Devon, where the Bedfords owned a lot of land and kept a smaller property, Endsleigh Cottage, which lent its name, of course, to the street in which Levy resided in the 1880s. The grounds of Endsleigh Cottage, nestling in the idyllic Tamar Valley, were landscaped to a design by Sir Humphry Repton in 1809, a few years after he had laid down the gardens of Russell Square. This was Bloomsbury's largest patch of green to survive the rapid speculative development in the latter decades of the eighteenth and first few decades of the nineteenth centuries.

To residents born in the 1800s, for whom the area was as built-up as it is today, Victorian Bloomsbury's semi-rural past appears to have been the source of uncanny wonder or bemusement. It is in that spirit that Charles Dickens's historical novel about the Gordon Riots, *Barnaby Rudge* (1841), draws attention to the fields of Bloomsbury in 1780. In this rural Bloomsbury he situates the pub that serves as the rioters' headquarters: 'This Boot was a lone house of public entertainment, situated in the fields at the back of the Foundling Hospital; a very solitary spot at that period, and quite deserted after dark. The tavern stood at some distance from any high road, and was approachable only by a dark and narrow lane.'[4]

The Boot is an actual pub that can be found today on Cromer Street, rebuilt in 1801 on the site of the original, which was properly called the Golden Boot. In the eighteenth century, this was a semi-rural inn complete with a tearoom, attracting Londoners in search of something approaching country air, and perhaps a game of skittles. George Cattermole's illustrations to the novel emphasise the bucolic quaintness of the eighteenth-century

George Cattermole, 'The Rioters Headquarters'. Plate from Charles Dickens, *Barnaby Rudge*, Biographical Edition, 1902 (with plates after the original illustrations). Cattermole's illustration of the Boot pub emphasises the rural location of Bloomsbury at the time of the Gordon Riots.

original, drawing on the same kind of picturesque aesthetic that inspired John Constable's *The Hay Wain* (1817) – which was painted, incidentally, in Bloomsbury, when England's greatest landscape painter lived in Keppel Street (the house was demolished to make way for Senate House). In Cattermole's hands the illustration's title, *The Rioters' Headquarters*, is clearly meant to resonate ironically with its idyllic composition of thatch, fencing, tree and pond.

In the late 1830s, when he started planning *Barnaby Rudge*, Dickens was living in a house in Doughty Street, where the Dickens House Museum is now located. He would have known the modern, urbanised Boot, and felt the contrast it made with the eighteenth-century Golden Boot that it replaced. In making its previous, rural iteration such an integral part of his novel, and in having Cattermole devote one of a limited number of illustrations to its depiction, he seems to have wanted to mark the enormous changes his local neighbourhood had undergone in a matter of sixty years.

Intriguingly, the memory of Bloomsbury's green past was kept alive for the whole of the nineteenth century through the circulation of a kind of ghost story that drew attention to the grounds upon which the neighbourhood's streets and squares came to be constructed. Gaining fame firstly in the eighteenth century through an oral tale, the story revolves around part of Montague Fields, behind Montague House (an area that housed the British Museum from 1759 until the 1840s). A doubly fatal duel between brothers fighting on different sides of the Civil War was said to have led to the implacable inscription of forty mysterious footprints upon the ground where they fought, footprints within which no grass could grow.

In the eighteenth century, the 'forty footsteps' tale mustered enough currency to attract a kind of ghost tourism to this part of green Bloomsbury. The poet Robert Southey was one of

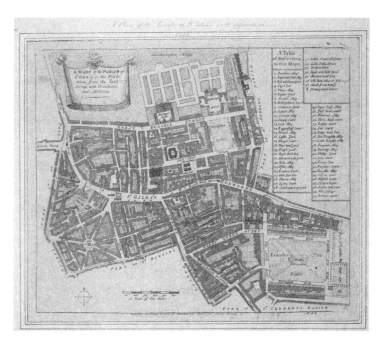

A Plan of the Parish of St Giles as it appeared in 1755. Published according to Act of Parliament 1755 for Stow's Survey. Montague House, Bedford House and Bloomsbury Square are clearly depicted in the top third of the map.

the more well-known pilgrims to see the footsteps for himself. In the nineteenth century, when the haunted site had only recently been covered by buildings and roads, the story found renewed life via a novel by Jane Porter, entitled *The Field of Forty Footsteps* (1828). Its first chapter describes the narrator's investigation of the pilgrimage destination at first hand. It is worth quoting extensively, inscribing as it does what in some way can be seen as a kind of founding mythology for modern Bloomsbury. Note the way the new university – engine of Enlightenment rationality – rises with its 'populous colonnades' to block out the rural feudal past that is symbolised by those residual footprints:

> I set forth one fine sunny morning last April [1827], accompanied by my friend, to explore what traces might yet remain of the field itself . . . Starting from Bedford Square, and walking up Southampton Row, we struck off at the given point, which, in our guide's time, led directly into the country. Our first step thence was at once into Russell Square. We could not pause a moment to observe how differently the eye computes distance, when stretching over the free expanse of natural ground, from what it would calculate when that ground is partitioned out into the various obstructing appearances of town. Here, stone pavement, railed parterre, and fine houses on every side, had completely usurped the place of pasture fields, with their sheep and kine. The former more extensive rural prospect, spreading to the sky-met hills beyond, was totally excluded . . .
>
> We moved on . . . reach[ing] the new street called Upper Montague Street. It runs due north from the square; and just athwart its farther extremity, where it is unfinished, we perceived a rough sort of temporary paling, and an openness beyond which promised some vestige of the former country . . . to our great delight, [we] beheld a space that had evidently been part of the Long Fields; a large irregular tract of ground, but sorely disfigured from its described state of pastoral freshness and beauty. Near the paling all was entirely deprived of verdure; lime and other building cements having quite discoloured the surface. And further on, on

every side, the soil was cut up by foundations for houses; and spotted over with heaps of rubbish, bricks, logs of timber, workmen's sheds, and other objects of active masonry.

But, on viewing the yet unbuilt-on space more distinguishingly, we discerned, towards the centre of the quarter nighest to where we stood, and about a stone's throw forward, that the earth retained its vernal sod; being covered there with a short and thick, though scrubby grass; and that it extended in like manner to a pretty considerable stretch of field equally green, excepting on a few barren surfaces of oblong shapes, lying in waving positions on a continuation of the oblique line we had pursued across the ground, and at regular paces distant, till they were hidden from our further observation by some hurdles and a tool-house . . .

'There they are!' we exclaimed in a breath, while both pointed at the same moment to the last traces of what we verily believed to be the marks we came to seek . . . and we stood gazing on the remnants of that earth-record, as if we could have read there the awful cry, 'Remember!' once uttered over them . . .

[O]nly a few days after we had thus recognised them, the first stone of the New London University was laid, at the north-western extremity of this only remaining remnant of the Long Fields; and in a spot not less belonging to the story of the tradition than the particular field of the memorable marks itself.

On that very spot, where the scaffolding for the new erection now stands, about two centuries ago stood an old family country-seat, with its courts and gardens, and high-pinnacled roof, and turret windows, over-topping a lofty avenue of elms, which led from that side of the mansion into the noted field. But it will be seen the story of that field swept all the rest away; the mansion, and its courts, and its gardens, as though they had never been; and the green herbage of the depopulated domain, afterwards called the Long Fields, waved over the site of the whole . . .

And now the time is arrived when the mysterious memorial itself shall be as entirely gone; when the halls and the gardens of the intended great establishment may, even before the first anniversary of its foundation comes round, have effaced every blade of grass from the once awfully-regarded spot, and buried its scathed marks under populous colonnades . . .[5]

While the construction of the university is said to have 'effaced every blade of grass' memorialised in this local legend, there are thankfully still many lawns on which one may plant one's own footmarks. In the last ten or fifteen years, a lottery-funded project has worked to restore a number of the gardens so that they more closely resemble those that the squares' first inhabitants would have encountered; 1820s Bloomsbury may have been haunted by its rural past, but today it appears to be nostalgic for the cultivated gardens of its nineteenth century.

Three of these squares are particularly worth a visit by garden lovers today – Gordon, Tavistock and Russell. While its centre still includes formal beds, Gordon Square otherwise enjoys a relatively relaxed horticultural affect, which chimes well with its social vibe on sunny summer evenings when students laze around there after a day's lectures. Ivy is left to climb some of the trees, providing habitats for wildlife less frequently found in other urban parks. The south-west corner has been left more or less undisturbed, and sports woodland ground flora such as bluebells, cow parsley and dog violets. The gardens of Tavistock Square, meanwhile, include a number of trees to commemorate different wars. Prime of these is the bird cherry (*Prunus padus*), which blossoms spectacularly in spring with unusually dense clusters of flowers. Dedicated to the victims of Hiroshima, the tree joins a pair of works of public art deployed in the cause of pacifism – a statue of Mahatma Gandhi, and the Conscientious Objectors' Commemorative Stone. Around this triptych of objects, annual ceremonies calling for world peace take place.

If Tavistock Square has accrued an important role in remembering and decrying the horror of military history, Russell Square is the most notable in terms of garden history. When Repton was hired to landscape the gardens, he introduced a romantic spirit, with curving paths and lots of blossoming limes – a design to which the current model is fairly faithful.

FRANCIS
DUKE OF BEDFORD.

Richard Westmacott's statue of Francis Russell, 5th Duke of Bedford, in Russell Square. Erected in 1807, the statue portrays the Duke as an agriculturalist, with one hand on a plough and a sheep at his feet.

Nineteenth-century engraving of a Punch and Judy show in Russell Square. *Drawn by Tho. H. Shepherd Engraved by C. Motram.* The statue of Francis Russell overlooks proceedings.

At the southern side of Russell Square is a very different kind of memorial from those in Tavistock Square. A statue of one of the past landowners, Francis Russell, holds ears of corn in one hand while the other rests on a plough. Like King George III, the fifth Duke of Bedford was famed for the unusual interest he took in agriculture and agricultural improvement, maintaining a large model farm at his country estate. Apart from the names of the squares themselves, the statue is a rare reminder of the feudal land ownership system that, despite Bloomsbury's modernity, has underwritten the neighbourhood's history even up to the present. While the Bedford estate once covered nearly half of Bloomsbury's entire land mass and was the landlord for the majority of its tenants, even now, though much diminished, it maintains considerable holdings there.

Most of the Bloomsbury gardens themselves transferred into public ownership in the mid-twentieth century. In the nineteenth century, however, these squares were private and inaccessible to the general public. Although Russell Square's only sculpture is a statue of a past landowner, the part it played in radical histories could easily justify something less reactionary. The largest Chartist march – of 1848 – started in Russell Square and ended in Kennington Common. Less well known is the fact that Russell Square was significant in the democratisation of London's green space (long before these sites' ownership transferred to the local council) because of the pioneering flower shows held there from the 1860s onwards. Inviting for the first time hordes of working-class people into one of London's private garden squares, the Bloomsbury Flower Show allowed poor local residents to exhibit the geraniums they had grown on their window sills in a space to which they normally had no access. An event with such a mixed demographic, in a location that was usually so exclusive, seemed outlandish to many contemporaries, as the tone of this report from the *City Press* suggests: 'The inhabitants of

Russell-square have consented to allow the exhibition of their garden, which sounds as if the end of the world were near at hand.'[6]

If the 'end of the world' in this context approximated to the transfer of Bloomsbury's squares into the public realm, the journalist needn't have been so worried, as that catastrophe wouldn't happen for another eighty years.

The provision of Bloomsbury's green space to its working-class population did improve before this, though. Bloomsbury was the site of one of Octavia Hill's first campaigns for 'London Gardens for the Poor', namely St George's Gardens, tucked behind the Foundling Museum. Hill's Kyrle Society advocated on behalf of those excluded from public space, seeking to increase the amount of it available to poor people by safeguarding current wasteland from the march of speculative builders, and transforming it into new parks and gardens. Here is her begging letter, dated 1883, to the editor of the *Standard*:

SIR, – The Trustees of the disused burial-ground at St. George's, Bloomsbury, are willing to hand it over in perpetuity to St. Pancras Vestry. The Vestry will maintain it, provide caretakers, and open it to the public, as soon as it shall have been put in order and laid out as a garden . . .

The sooner these closed wildernesses of churchyards are set in order, handed over to the local authorities, and opened to the public, the better. Hidden by walls, covered with rubbish, closed to the inhabitants of the stifling courts in their neighbourhood, if they are not rescued for those who live near them they may become the prey of the commercial speculator or the railway company.

We are most of us now planning where we will go for the summer holidays. If there are any who wish to leave behind them a gift which shall help to provide quiet, space, green grass, trees, and fresh air for those to whom successive years bring no visits to mountains or sea, will they send donations to this garden?[7]

View of St George's Gardens. Evidence of its role as a burial ground can be seen against the wall. Opening in 1714, the burial ground was one of the first to be created in open country, away from the church it served. In 1884, by now much closer to the centre of the sprawling metropolis, it opened as St George's Gardens, a public space for the poorer Bloomsbury residents.

According to the Scottish botanist Charles Loudon, Repton had deliberately designed Russell Square's gardens with the space towards the edges open and comparatively unplanted, in order that parents living in the surrounding houses could supervise their children by keeping an eye on them from their drawing-room windows. For less fortunate younger residents of the area, from the poorer parts of the district, St George's Gardens would prove a valuable playground.

From the foundation of the Foundling Hospital onwards, Bloomsbury had been associated with the care of children and the 'cultivation' of youth. Bloomsbury's role in introducing the Kindergarten movement to Britain likewise draws together the two themes of this chapter – youth and the natural world – through the evocatively metaphorical character of its name. From 1853, 32 Tavistock Place was the base from which two German political refugees, Johannes and Bertha Ronge, disseminated the liberal pedagogical theory behind their 'gardens for children', which derived from the pioneering work of Friedrich Froebel. Emphasising the value of non-didactic play for child development in a way that contrasted significantly with standard Victorian educational models, horticulture was not only a metaphor. An actual garden was, in fact, a crucial part of the Bloomsbury kindergarten. Cultivating plants was one of the ways in which children were encouraged to learn experientially and 'grow' personally.

The image of the ailing flower as a metaphor for fragile youth became specifically associated with Bloomsbury soon after the establishment of Great Ormond Street's Children's Hospital in 1852, when Charles Dickens and Henry Morley co-wrote an article in the latter's periodical, *Household Words*, entitled 'Drooping Buds':

> What should we say of a rose-tree in which one bud out of every three dropped to the soil dead? We should not say that this was natural to roses; neither is it natural to men and women that they

should see the glaze of death upon so many of the bright eyes that come to laugh and love among them or that they should kiss so many little lips grown cold and still. The vice is external. We fail to prevent disease; and, in the case of children, to a much more lamentable extent than is well known, we fail to cure it.

Like the Ronges' institute nearby, the provision of an actual garden was seen to be important in a modern institution dedicated to the care of children. Indeed, Dickens's piece specifically asked for money to be able to set about making this happen:

> the space generally is very ample, and is at present a mere wilderness. The funds of the hospital have only sufficed to authorise the occupation of a building, and the preparation for a great useful work. For means to plant the roses in the garden, and to plant the roses in the cheeks of many children besides those who come under their immediate care, the Hospital Committee has support to find . . . Is it too much to believe that the little beds in the great house will never be suffered to remain empty, while there are little shapes of pain and unrest to lie down in them; or that the wilderness in the garden will be taught to bloom with recovered infant health?[8]

Dickens was not the only writer to lend his eloquence to the cause of this famous institution. In 1937, when J. M. Barrie died, his will dictated that the copyright funds accruing from posthumous productions of his play *Peter Pan* should go to Great Ormond Street Children's Hospital. A reliable slew of pantomimes each year, not to mention the odd successful film adaptation, has meant that Barrie's legacy has continued to fund children's care quite substantially (although its chief source of income is now, of course, the NHS).

'Mrs Dalloway said she would buy the flowers herself.' Thus begins that most famous of all Bloomsbury novels, *Mrs Dalloway* (1925), a novel that appeared not long after its author had moved

The Hours

Chapter One.

Oct 20th
1924

Mrs Dalloway said she would buy the flowers herself...

Manuscript page for the opening paragraphs of Virginia Woolf's *Mrs Dalloway*, published in 1925.

back to the neighbourhood. It was at 52 Tavistock Square that Virginia Woolf wrote much of her most important fiction, all of which was published by the Hogarth Press – the small printing house that the novelist and her husband Leonard ran from the basement of their Bloomsbury home. Woolf's experience of Bloomsbury in the 1920s was a highly fertile time, one budding forth with new ideas. At the same time, *Mrs Dalloway* is a terribly sad novel, which culminates in the suicide of Septimus Smith, the shell-shocked soldier who has returned, traumatised, to civilian life.

Read with this tragic climax in mind, the memorable opening sentence might suggest the *flos campi* (flowers of the field) – a phrase much used at the time to signal the mass graves of young men mown down in the fields of Flanders. Like the famous paintings of stark tree stumps in war-torn landscapes by Paul Nash (who studied at the Slade School of Art, part of UCL, and lived opposite St Pancras station in the 1920s), Woolf's novel uses an image from the natural world subtly to gesture to the industrialised youth mortality rates that the war had recently produced.

Budding flowers remind us both of new life and of its fragility; of ephemerality; of mortality. This tells us something about Bloomsbury too. Like her friend Eleanor Marx, Amy Levy, the poet of Bloomsbury in bud, committed suicide, at the tragically early age of twenty-seven. Levy had just received proofs for the collection in which the poem was published, *A London Plane-Tree*, when she gassed herself in her rooms. Another fine female Bloomsbury poet to take her own life, in 1928, was Charlotte Mew. One of her finest poems, 'The Trees are Down' (1920) was written after she saw, near her house in Gordon Street, the plane trees opposite Euston station cut down in order to widen the main road. Like Levy in 'The London Plane-Tree', Mew seems to identify Bloomsbury's natural world with a fresh, youthful sense of 'spring' and, moreover, identifies herself with that youthful spring in jeopardy.

—and he cried with a loud voice:
Hurt not the earth, neither the sea, nor the trees—
(Revelation)

They are cutting down the great plane-trees at the end of the
   gardens.
For days there has been the grate of the saw, the swish of the
   branches as they fall,
The crash of the trunks, the rustle of trodden leaves,
With the 'Whoops' and the 'Whoas,' the loud common talk,
   the loud common laughs of the men, above it all.

I remember one evening of a long past Spring
Turning in at a gate, getting out of a cart, and finding a large
   dead rat in the mud of the drive.
I remember thinking: alive or dead, a rat was a god-forsaken
   thing,
But at least, in May, that even a rat should be alive.

The week's work here is as good as done. There is just one bough
   On the roped bole, in the fine grey rain,
      Green and high
      And lonely against the sky.
       (Down now!—)
      And but for that,
      If an old dead rat
Did once, for a moment, unmake the Spring, I might never
   have thought of him again.

It is not for a moment the Spring is unmade to-day;
These were great trees, it was in them from root to stem:
When the men with the 'Whoops' and the 'Whoas' have carted
   the whole of the whispering loveliness away
Half the Spring, for me, will have gone with them.

It is going now, and my heart has been struck with the hearts
   of the planes;
Half my life it has beat with these, in the sun, in the rains,

In the March wind, the May breeze,
In the great gales that came over to them across the roofs from
the great seas.
There was only a quiet rain when they were dying;
They must have heard the sparrows flying,
And the small creeping creatures in the earth where they were
lying—
But I, all day, I heard an angel crying:
'Hurt not the trees.'[9]

"'Bloomsbury Cathedral': The Catholic Apostolic Church in Gordon Square.' Photograph in St John Adcock (ed), *Wonderful London*, 1928.

Chapter 2   **Aspiring**

From the moment in the 1820s that the new University College (UCL) was branded 'the godless college of Gower Street',[1] in response to its lack of a theology department or a chapel, Bloomsbury has been defined by its secularism. If God died sometime in the nineteenth century, as many philosophers since Nietzsche have argued, His absence appears to have made itself felt more swiftly in this neighbourhood than elsewhere. It is an appropriate irony in this light that the most gargantuan and grand of Bloomsbury's churches, the Church of Christ the King on Gordon Square, is defined by a part of its design that is palpably missing.

Constructed in the 1850s to house the congregation of an unusual charismatic-ritualist sect called the Catholic Apostolic Church, led by the famous preacher Edward Irving, the church's architect Raphael Brandon designed a space large enough to rival cathedrals, but the project run out of money before the dream could be fully realised. The spire of Brandon's church was originally intended to be 300 feet high, which would have made it the tallest spire in London by far. As it is, still nestled immediately behind the thriving secular university, the Church of Christ the King makes do with a somewhat embarrassing stump of a tower, which cannot help but declare its failure to make good upon over-ambitious aspirations.

The tallest spire actually to materialise in the neighbourhood was not for a church at all. It graces the clock tower of Gilbert

'The Magnificent Frontage of St. Pancras, the Midland Railway Terminus in London', in Frederick Arthur Ambrose Talbot, *Railway Wonders of the World*, Cassell 1913–14.

Scott's railway hotel for St Pancras station, to the immediate north of Bloomsbury. When, in Thomas Hardy's *Jude the Obscure* (1895), Sue Bridehead says she prefers railways stations to cathedrals, the novelist may well have been thinking of this building, whose design famously blurred the line between the two kinds of institution. The gothic red-brick enormity on the Euston Road was very quickly called by critics a 'cathedral of modernity', largely because of its multiple spires.

Before Hardy became a writer he had trained to be an architect, and in the 1860s, in the run-up to the construction of St Pancras station, he was employed to oversee the removal of graves from Old St Pancras churchyard. This odd task is the subject of a poem he wrote over a decade later, 'The Levelled Graveyard' (1882). Two verses read:

> O passenger, pray list and catch
> Our sighs and piteous groans,
> Half stifled in this jumbled patch
> Of wrenched memorial stones!
>
> We late-lamented, resting here,
> Are mixed to human jam,
> And each to each exclaims in fear,
> 'I know not which I am!'[2]

Voicing the complaint of one of the souls whose remains have been moved to make way for the new railway, the poem plays with the form of a prayer. It ends, desperately, with the word 'AMEN', in a vain hope that some final resting place might be found amidst the flux of secular urban modernity. But, sardonically, it is the (railway) 'passenger' to whom this prayer is addressed – the mobile consumer as God. St Pancras may have been called a cathedral of modernity because of its spires, but Hardy here subtly teases out the implications of the building's blatant appropriation of the formal language of ecclesiastical architecture for secular purposes.

Entrance hall in Senate House. Constructed between 1932 and 1937, this art deco building was designed by architect Charles Holden, best known at the time for his modernist work on London Underground stations.

Although nowadays other parts of London have overtaken the West Central district in this respect, for much of the twentieth century Bloomsbury was associated with unusually tall buildings. Extending into the sky as if bidding for perfection, the neighbourhood's 'skyscrapers' mimicked the spires and church towers of previous eras. In the 1930s Charles Holden completed his Senate House, the site of the administrative offices and library of the University. Its 209-feet-high tower was the tallest secular building in London, after the Houses of Parliament. Holden had previously made a name for himself through his designs for the London Underground, and the skyscraper he built at the end of Store Street was every bit as modern as his work for that infrastructural project. Aping contemporaneous American structures, Senate House was the first edifice of such proportions in the UK that was designed to run on electricity for its heating, and the chief public rooms were even treated to an early form of air conditioning. Underlining the extreme modernity of Holden's building, Sir William Beveridge, former Vice-Chancellor, said that Senate House was 'something that could not have been built by any earlier generation than this, and can only be at home in London'.[3]

When in 1966 George Marsh's 34-storey Centre Point was completed at Bloomsbury's south-western corner, at the bottom of Tottenham Court Road, it dwarfed Senate House, not to mention many of the other buildings in the locality. Rising to 385 feet, Marsh's building quickly attracted negative attention from critics, to a large degree because it was constructed in a property boom for use as office space – and then stood empty for several years while its owner waited for a lucrative deal with a single tenant. Occupied in 1974 by housing activists, including the current Labour MP Jack Dromey, Centre Point became the central target of a kind of politicised architectural critique of the hubris and hollowness of such socially ill-employed tall buildings in the midst of a housing crisis. The kind of critique provoked by Centre Point has witnessed a revival in the last decade or so,

Centre Point, 101–103 New Oxford Street. Constructed from 1963 to 1966, the building was one of the first skyscrapers in London. Since 1995 Centre Point has been a Grade II listed building, and in 2015 it was converted from office space to luxury flats.

with the epidemic of skyscrapers that have sprung up in many parts of London, such as the Shard at London Bridge.

The severe negative criticism from various quarters that was attracted by the Senate House and Centre Point reflected the specific concerns of the decades of their respective constructions. But both structures were also decried for the same reason – that their sheer scale dwarfed church buildings in the locality, and blocked views from other parts of the city of the ecclesiastical content of London's skyline. It appears that, for a number of commentators, the sheer height of such tall secular buildings, whether academic or commercial, threatened the churches and cathedrals in their shadow, not merely by physically dwarfing them but also by implicitly parodying them.

Bloomsbury's built environment has an overt linearity that can be witnessed not only in its once very unusual skyscrapers, but also in the horizontal plan of the area. Laid out in a kind of grid system, Bloomsbury cannot conceal it is the product of human design. Unlike its eastern neighbour of Clerkenwell, whose windy medieval lanes burrow below its subsequent architecture as if the place had organic roots, Bloomsbury's street plan trialled the straight lines and sharp corners that would later be brought to fruition more extremely in places like Manhattan. Urban historians such as Donald Olsen have argued that the neighbourhood – largely built as a prominent speculative project over a few decades between 1770 and 1820, rather than emerging haphazardly over the centuries – should be recognised as a successful pioneer of town planning. In the nineteenth century it was fashionable to decry how boringly uniform were the long straight roads such as Gower Street, but we might instead appreciate this total linearity as an essential part of Bloomsbury's architectural character, by the way it embodies the logic of modernity.

Bloomsbury was, after all, the location of the first specially designed open space in London to be called a square. Initially

'North Front of Bedford House, Bloomsbury Square.' Engraving based on a drawing that was purchased at a sale at Bedford House. R. Wilkinson 1822. Bedford House was demolished in 1800 to make way for the construction of Bedford Place and Montague Street.

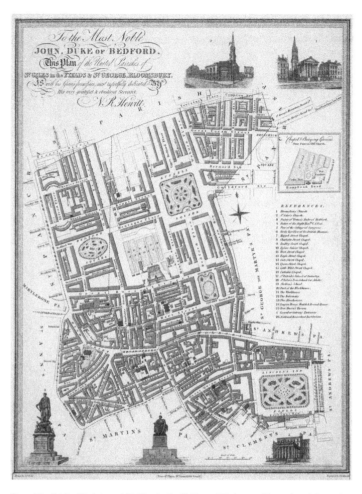

Plan of the 'United Parishes of St. Giles in the Fields and St George, Bloomsbury'. Drawn by J. Wyld and engraved and published by N. R. Hewitt 1824.

known as Southampton Square, what is now called Bloomsbury Square was conceived in around 1647 when the Earl of Southampton had his town residence, Bedford House, rebuilt. This site provided a model not only for the other squares that emerged when the Bedfords redeveloped the area in earnest towards the end of the eighteenth century, but also for the hundreds built across the city in later years. The squares of Bloomsbury offer something more than the gift of *rus in urbe* signalled by their gardens. In the proportionate symmetry of their geometry and the ordered openness of their form, they might be seen to proclaim their aspirations towards a more perfectly enlightened, transparent, rational future.

Of course, Bloomsbury's straight lines and squares have at least as much to do with capitalism's functionalist preference for efficiency as for anything else, as an article about the area's recent development in the *Morning Chronicle* from 1826 betrays:

> The present nominal or apparent high interest afforded by the rent of houses, as compared with any other outlay of capital, still continues to throw enormous sums into the hands of the builders, and enables them to execute the most gigantic projects . . . raised as if architects had become possessed of the lamp of Aladdin. Taking the Strand as a centre, and looking north upon that space bounded by the New Road and Tottenham and Gray's Inn Roads, we are struck with astonishment to see the ground which, thirty years ago, formed the garden and meadows of Montague House, now covered with spacious and even magnificent houses, and laid out in squares and streets not to be surpassed, if they are equalled, by any portion of the metropolis.[4]

There is a tension in this passage between an acknowledgement of the material cause of Bloomsbury's sudden development – profit – and a genuine 'astonishment' at the 'magnificent' products themselves, which manifest themselves suddenly as if by magic. This tug between the material and the transcendent is, in a sense, intrinsic to the form of Bloomsbury's squares, paying homage as they do to the idea of the Agora, the public space at the heart of ancient Greek cities. In Athens the Agora was the site simultaneously of democratic deliberation, athletic display, religious ceremony and commercial exchange. Though matched by no means in the actual practices contained within Russell or Bedford Squares in the 1800s, Bloomsbury's multiple open spaces gestured to the Agora's richer, more ambitious mixture of public activities, which included the spiritual. Bespeaking at once the material aspirations of landowners and builders, who were capitalising on the unprecedented increase in London's land values after the Industrial Revolution, Bloomsbury's squares can also be seen to suggest a longing for the ideal.

Two totemic urban forms that were introduced to Bloomsbury before spreading to other parts of London – the skyscraper and the garden square – both announce within their different historical contexts a strong commitment to a kind of rationalist modernity. The form of each, however, also carries traces of transcendental idealism, discernible in the perfect symmetry of the latter and the heavenwards ascendancy of the former. Bloomsbury squares stand simultaneously as efficiently reproducible products for a speculative housing market, and homages to the Agora, with its spiritual connotations. The towers, meanwhile, represent the technological achievements of secular materialism and yet, at the same time, their forms also appear to express some kind of yearning for the celestial regions. This chapter explores a curious traffic between the secular and the religious within Bloomsbury's built environment, tracing the way its prominent buildings recapitulate the idealism of earlier traditions by the features they borrow from religious architecture.

The 'godless' college of UCL provides two particularly notable examples of this phenomenon. The Cruciform Building borrows the sign of the cross for the purpose of modern medicine. Today

Aerial photograph of the Cruciform Building, University College London, Gower Street.

it contains the university's medical libraries and accommodates many of the lectures provided to its trainee medics, but originally the building housed the North London Hospital (later known as University College Hospital), one of Bloomsbury's many important medical institutions. Constructed between 1896 and 1906 to a design by Alfred and Paul Waterhouse, the building's red-brick and terracotta gothic appears deliberately to stand in almost aggressive contrast with the grey classicism of William Wilkins's quadrangle which it faces on the other side of the north end of Gower Street.

The cross shape of the building was a solution simultaneously to problems of ventilation, drainage and lighting. Arranged in diagonal lines that jut against those of the street, the hospital's wards were identically sized, each containing twenty-eight beds. In order to raise funding for such an ambitious and ingeniously planned space, an appeal was launched to attract donations from the general public. This bore substantial fruit in the interest of the local Bloomsbury businessman and philanthropist, Sir John Blundell Maple, owner of the famous furniture store on Tottenham Court Road to the hospital's rear. He was reputedly so impressed with the architect's vision for the building that he provided an estimated £100,000 towards the financing of its construction and equipment.

The university's neoclassical portico and dome, meanwhile, quote the temples of ancient Greece as, indeed, do a number of buildings in Bloomsbury. William Wilkins was the architect for its keynote buildings from the 1820s, which were positioned around the main quadrangle. The entrance to the quadrangle can be found at the north end of Gower Street. Wilkins's Greek Revivalist neoclassical design echoes its near contemporary, the National Gallery, the design for which the architect was also responsible. An article from 1828 published in the *Gentleman's Magazine*, while the building was still under construction,

'University College, Gower Street' Plate from George Walter Thornbury, *Old and New London*, 1879–85.

reveals how Wilkins's projected university was dreamt to a scale even grander than the one that came to pass.

> The building, when finished, is to consist of a central portico, and two wings advancing at right angles, with tetratyle porticos to correspond. The central portico consists of ten columns of the Corinthian order, supporting an enriched entablature and pediment, sculptured with ornaments emblematic of the objects of the institution. Over the whole, and springing from the vestibule, will appear an elevated dome, surmounted by a Grecian temple of eight pillars. Over each wing corresponding domes of a smaller size will also appear.[5]

A shortfall in the budget was, predictably, the reason behind the failure in execution. The most impressive feature to materialise from the blueprint to Wilkins's partially realised *grand projet* was the vast dome, which had to be recast in 1848 due to faults in the initial engineering. Its high ceiling serves as a kind of canopy for the Flaxman Gallery, an octagonal space that exhibits work by John Flaxman, the leading British sculptor of the early nineteenth century. Of equal importance to the contents of the dome, however, is its shape and dimensions. Beyond any ornaments adorning the building's structure, the dome itself can be seen to bear witness to the progressive 'objects of the institution' at the time of its foundation. The second version of the dome for the Capitol building in Washington had just been completed, in 1823, only a few years before Wilkins's design. Domes in the early nineteenth century were thus associated with the secularism and separation of powers that was embodied by post-revolutionary America.

When the Gothic revivalist Augustus Pugin decried the new college's architecture as 'pagan', the dome would have been one of the key causes for his critique. Living nearby in 106 Great Russell Street, Pugin could not have ignored the contribution to the skyline made by the new 'godless college of Gower Street', rising spectacularly as its dome did then above Bloomsbury's townhouses. Of course Pugin's adjective 'pagan' referred to something missing from Wilkin's design as much as anything it included – namely, the absence of any church, chapel or other place of worship. Importantly, the new university set up a Professorship in Architecture, but not in Theology. University College had been founded as a non-denominational academic institution suitable for non-conformists, atheists and Jews, at a time when the doors to older universities such as Oxford and Cambridge remained closed to these constituencies by requiring its undergraduates to subscribe publically to the tenets of Anglicanism.

Ironically, however, for all its associations with the secularism of progressive revolutions in America and France, the dome that crowns University College could equally recall those that feature on great cathedrals and basilicas. For the novelist and artist George Du Maurier, who also lived in Great Russell Street (in the 1860s), the design of the college conjured a sense of the exotically religious. In his odd version of a science-fiction novel, *The Martian* (1897), the university's most prominent architectural feature seems to collude with some street music by transporting the narrator imaginatively from prosaic Bloomsbury to romantic Venice: 'A belated Italian organ-grinder stopped beneath us and played a tune from *I Lombardi*, called "La mia letizia" . . . Tavistock Square became a broad Venetian moonlit lagoon, and the dome of University College an old Italian church, and "La mia letizia" the song of Adria's gondolier.'[6]

Du Maurier's whimsical insistence on a resemblance between Wilkins's dome and that of a Venetian church gestures to a certain symbolic slipperiness about it, a slipperiness to which Pugin would have strongly objected. That one of the most notable architectural features of an avowedly secular modern university could be mistaken for a 'belated' ecclesiastical dome would have seemed a kind of architectural over-shoot, verging on blasphemy.

Nineteenth-century photograph of the construction of the British Museum's reading room.

'Novel View of the British Museum Surrounded by the Massed Trees of Bloomsbury.'
Photograph in St John Adcock (ed), *Wonderful London*, 1928.

Wilkins's dome for University College was an ambitious project for its time, but it was modest in comparison with the dome which would be completed a few decades later nearby at the British Museum. Still at the heart of what is the most visited tourist site in the UK, the circular reading room has housed a number of blockbuster exhibitions in recent years, having not acted as a library since it closed its doors to readers back in 2000. The building was designed by Sydney Smirke, and constructed between 1854 and 1857 in order to address a marked expansion of the collections of books, manuscripts and maps – not to mention an even greater increase in numbers of readers using these resources at the museum.

It was the determination of the Keeper of Printed Books at the time, Antonio Panizzi, that there should be a round room in the central courtyard, and it was largely this Italian exile's appeals to Parliament that persuaded the nation to find the funds to make this huge construction project a reality. Panizzi's youth had been spent in fighting for political progress in his own country, and the circular shape of the room he envisioned bears witness to the universal democratic values he wished to inscribe into the new building as a legacy of his custodianship of the library.

The British Museum may have had the idea of national identity built into its mission, by virtue of its name, but for Panizzi, the new reading room could also signal that Britishness need not preclude a sense of the global or the cosmopolitan. On the vast level floor a series of attractive desk-rows spread from a central point towards the circumference in concentric rings. Three hundred readers could thus be accommodated simultaneously, each reader being afforded a separate table of ample depth, furnished with a convenient reading-stand plus a shelf for books of reference. In formation, they might seem to make up one round table, an image of the *cosmopolis*, for citizens of everywhere.

'The Book-Cases at the British Museum.' Plate from George Walter Thornbury, *Old and New London*, 1879–85.

The space wowed many critics at the time, such as a reviewer from *Leisure Hour*, who marvelled at 'the largest circular-domed edifice in the whole world, with the single exception of that of the Pantheon in Rome – a building which men of science will come from far to see, and which may be the admiration of generations yet unborn'.[7] Those men of science would have made their pilgrimage to marvel at this building's technological advancements as much as anything else. With a diameter of 42.6 metres the dome may have recalled those of the ancient world, but the building was also the epitome of modernity, through its innovations in ventilation and heating, and in its deployment of the most advanced building materials – cast iron, concrete and glass. Book stacks surrounding the reading room were constructed out of iron to add fire protection, as well as to take the huge weight of the dome itself.

The *Leisure Hour's* review goes into great detail about all aspects of the space, at floor level, gradually raising its eyes upwards, but is particularly transfixed when it comes to describing the dome:

From the projecting cornice above the third tier of bookshelves, the magnificent dome takes its forward spring, the several compartments, twenty in number, meeting in a handsome circular skylight, at a height of over a hundred feet. Each compartment contained an arched window, twenty-seven feet high and twelve in width, and these together with the central lantern above supply such an abundance of light, as would be looked for in vain in any private dwelling. It is owing to this abundance of light, perhaps, that the feeling of which one is often conscious while reading in the new room is mainly due. We allude to the idea which we have often heard expressed, that while sitting there one feels out of doors, and would not be surprised, at the end of an interesting chapter, to find one's self sitting in a field or forest under a tree . . .

'Reading Room of the Great Library at the British Museum Seen from Over the Entrance.'
Photograph in St John Adcock [ed], *Wonderful London*, 1928.

More than anything else, the dome meant an almost miraculous light – a luminosity distributed equally to all readers, and to a degree more intense than that available within even the grandest of private homes. The dome thus constituted an argument in material form about the possibilities for the Enlightenment supported by an enlarged public realm, but it also recapitulated an idealist symbolism it had derived from millennia of religious traditions. In his preface to *Conversations in Bloomsbury*, the Indian activist and writer Mulk Raj Anand, a Hindu, recalls 'eating sandwiches and feeding pigeons by the Corinthian pillars of our Mecca at the time'. He consciously points out the symbolic hybridity in play in a building like the British Museum, a place of secular pilgrimage for scholars of all faiths and none whose architecture quotes the temples of the Ancients.[8]

Interestingly, the tendency of Bloomsbury's avowedly secular institutions to quote from, and aspire to, the sublimities of religious buildings is echoed in the way a couple of its most notable Christian churches clearly borrow from the architectural language of other cultural traditions. Before the construction of the grand porticos of University College and the British Museum, the early nineteenth century's recommitment to ancient Hellenic architectural ideals was announced in Bloomsbury with the construction, between 1818 and 1822, of St Pancras New Church, which can be found on the corner of Euston Road and Southampton Row. This was the first of several London churches around this time to be built in the Greek Revival style. E. V. Lucas, in commenting upon the church's stylistic identity, also draws attention to the geographical opposition of railway station and church on either side of the Euston Road:

As Aubrey Beardsley, the marvellous youth who perished in his decadence, used to say, Euston station made it unnecessary to visit Egypt. I would not add that St Pancras Church makes it unnecessary to visit Greece; but it is a very interesting summary of Greek traditions; its main building being an adaptation of the Ionic temple of the Erectheion on the Acropolis at Athens, its tower deriving from the Horologium or Temple of the Winds, and its dependencies, with their noble caryatides, being adaptations of the south portico of the Pandroseion, also at Athens.[9]

At least some of the building's design appears to have been inspired not by Athens itself, but by the controversial Athenian objects recently rehoused in the British Museum – namely the Parthenon marbles. The columns that propped up the west galleries, for example, were allegedly copied directly from the marbles by the architects, William Inwood and his son Henry.

The church quickly became fashionable for the liberal and enlightened, and has been described as 'the parish church, par excellence, of Regency England'.[10] By 1864 the church had become recognised as an important site of church music upon the national scene, the composer Henry Smart becoming organist there. Neglected now, though highly admired at the time, Smart memorialised his Bloomsbury days through the local topographical name that he bestowed upon one of his hymn tunes, still much in circulation today – 'Regent Square'. This refers to another Greek Revivalist Bloomsbury church, which was built by the Inwoods in the 1820s, suffered bomb damage in the Blitz, and was subsequently demolished. One of the poems most frequently sung to this tune (the words are by John Mason Neale) opens with lyrics that employ construction as a metaphor: 'Christ is made the sure foundation / Christ the head and cornerstone'. In the nineteenth century, in fashionable new Bloomsbury churches such as St Pancras New and Regent Square with their resemblance to an ancient temple to Athena more than the cathedrals of the medieval past, congregations might have needed to be reminded of the 'foundation' of their worship.

Nineteenth-century print of St Pancras New Church.

Athena is, among other things, the goddess of music. An influential building that pays homage through its design to the Parthenon, it is perhaps appropriate that St Pancras New Church continues to maintain a key role in promoting and organising the composition of contemporary choral music. Coordinating the London Contemporary Church Music Festival since it was founded in 2002, the church has been responsible for commissioning pieces from some of the most famous figures writing choral music today, such as Michael Berkeley, Michael Finnissy, Gabriel Jackson and Cecilia McDowall. It also solicits composition from new, unknown talent, through an open Call for Scores. Thus far it has seen over eighty world premieres.

St Pancras New Church was commissioned in 1818, after a million pounds had been allocated from the national purse for the building of fifty new churches. This '50 Churches Bill' mimicked a Bill which Queen Anne had initiated a century earlier – a project that resulted in a structure in Bloomsbury which borrows not only from ancient Greece but also from a host of other architectural traditions. Nicholas Hawksmoor's design for the parish church of St George's, Bloomsbury, has delighted and puzzled visitors ever since the building was constructed, between 1716 and 1731. One of only twelve new churches actually to materialise from the over-ambitious total of fifty, commissioned in response to the steady growth of the post-Great Fire city, St George's has gone down in the history of ecclesiastical architecture as both an experimental anomaly and a masterpiece of the English baroque. Some of its remarkable eccentricities can be read as resourceful solutions to practical problems, while others are clearly flourishes of the extravagant signature of an artist in his prime.

Compared with the other London churches that Hawksmoor designed following the same Queen Anne commission, the space allotted for Bloomsbury's new place of worship was

'St. George's Church Bloomsbury'. Plate from George Walter Thornbury, *Old and New London*, 1879–85.

extremely limited. Not only was it awkwardly sandwiched between existing buildings, but the orientation of the plot posed a major challenge in that its longer side ran north–south rather than east–west. Tradition and theological teaching dictates that Christian churches include a long nave running from the west, where the baptismal font is usually found, to the east, where the altar is almost invariably positioned. In order to preserve the traditional orientation of the church and to avoid the ugly disproportion of a short, fat nave, Hawksmoor found a way to solve the problem of St George's shape by designing the new church so that, to those within, it appears to be a perfect cube with the altar in an apse to the east.

In reality the church is not quite a cube, as the north end of this pseudo-symmetrical space conceals a vestry behind pillars and a screen. As a carefully produced illusion Hawksmoor's cuboid nave is fascinating, and not only because it enabled his church to 'square' ecclesiastical tradition with mainstream taste. Hawksmoor was a Freemason at a time when Freemasonry might be understood as an expression of Enlightenment intellectual cosmopolitanism as much as anything else. In the geometrical oddity of St George's many scholars have recognised an architectural embodiment of early eighteenth-century Freemasonry's deistic pluralism, with the shape of the building paying homage not only to Solomon's Temple in Jerusalem, but also to other forms of non-Christian religious architecture, such as the Islamic mosque. A much more explicit reference to other, geographically distant, religious traditions can be seen in the church tower, which sports a pyramid with a statue of George I dressed as a Roman emperor on the top. The model for this peculiar ornament – which was embellished further in the nineteenth century – was the Mausoleum at Halicarnassus, descriptions of which Hawksmoor had become obsessed with as a young architect working under Christopher Wren. To have a king at the head of a church steeple is peculiar indeed, especially

Interior view of St George's Church, Bloomsbury, as it appears today.

after the 1688 Glorious Revolution, which had come to a messy accommodation about the limits of monarchy.

The compounded eccentricities of St George's hybrid symbolism have given rise to a number of theories, and many have sought to form patterns from its mixture of styles in order to solve the building as though it were an enigma or a conspiracy. In Peter Ackroyd's *Hawksmoor* (1985), St George's church forms (along with other London churches completed by the architect) one of the points of a pentagram that he is inscribing secretly upon the body of the city. In his narration, material instructions for the construction of St George's are mixed up with a kind of faux-Masonic, faux-Satanic hocus-pocus, which is locked away from general view in parentheses:

> We desire the Honble. Board to know that the Walls of the *Blooms-bury Church* are complete and all is prepar'd for the Plaisterers; it will be proper that they begin the Ceilings and Walls during the best of the Winter, that the Work be thoroughly dry before any Frost take it. The Church is bounded by Russell Street to the North, Queen Street to the West, and to the South-east Bloomsbury Market; this area being very populous in the months of Summer, the Fields being close by, what Preparations are to be made for outside Doors so that the Church may be shut from the Rabble? The West Tower is advanc'd about 25 or 28 Feet above the Roof of the Church, and I will place upon that my Historical Pillar which will be of square Form and built with rough Stone. (And this I do not add: on the Apex of this Shaft will be placed the seven-edged Starre which is the Eye of God. The Emperour Constantine set up a Pillar at Rome as big as this, in one Stone, and placed the Sunne on the Sumit of it. But that *parhelion* of false Sunne was forced to leave Shining: my Fabrick will last 1000 yeares, and the Starre will not be extinguish'd.)[11]

A number of Bloomsbury's most notable buildings employ pure geometrical shapes with unusual prominence, making their confident claims upon urban space in a way that suggests the idealism maintaining the area's intellectual life. In Ackroyd's reading of Hawksmoor's church, the architect's uniquely eccentric design signals a will to transcend the 'Rabble' of the material world, and to commune instead with something eternal and celestial – the very 'Eye of God'. In its secular buildings, as much as religious, built-for institutions that are dedicated to a plethora of diverse ideas, Bloomsbury's architecture can be seen to share in this aspiration.

'The Doric Arch Leading to Euston Station.' Photograph in St John Adcock (ed), *Wonderful London*, 1928.

Chapter 3 **Connecting**

At the beginning of the twentieth century, the journalist and essayist E. V. Lucas said that Bloomsbury 'gives the lie to the poet's statement that East and West can never meet'.[1] Centrally positioned, between the frontiers of Gray's Inn Road and Tottenham Court Road, Bloomsbury serves to connect the old slum district of Clerkenwell to posh West London, a part of the city that becomes steadily more exclusive as one moves further towards Marylebone. Before the intense gentrification of the inner part of East London in the 1990s, Bloomsbury still operated as a kind of threshold, upon which socially distant parts of the city touched and blended. Today it is much more securely positioned nearer the centre rather than the edge of London's enlarged wealthy core, Britain's capital city having experienced an asset bubble as a side-effect of having skimmed capital from the world's financial markets. Clerkenwell is as full of wealthy City boys as Fitzrovia. Yet, Bloomsbury remains a hybrid neighbourhood with an economically diverse population, retaining one of the largest and most densely concentrated stocks of un-privatised social housing in central London. It is still characterised by social mixture, and by the unpredictable and sometimes incongruous relationships that can be formed out of the collisions and collusions that result from such local demographic heterogeneity.

A semi-detached member of the Bloomsbury Group, E. M. Forster famously enjoins us to 'Only Connect' and, in a sense, this phrase might stand as a motto for Bloomsbury's connectivity. Remarkable acts of connection within fiction set in Bloomsbury by members of the Bloomsbury Group bear out what Lucas says of the locality's mysterious powers in crossing divides. In his posthumously published gay novel *Maurice*, an episode set in Bloomsbury allows Forster's narrative to begin pushing back against the pessimistic track it had hitherto been treading. The British Museum is the site where the novel's blackmail plot is scotched, and where the possibility of a non-tragic ending to a cross-class homosexual relationship is first truly mooted. The climax of Woolf's *Mrs Dalloway*, meanwhile, imagines a scene in which the social-geographical divide between an alienated upper-middle-class Westminster hostess and a suicidal Tottenham Court Road working-class man is momentarily bridged. In the guise of the affecting image of a traumatised ex-soldier's body mangled on the neighbourhood's railings, Bloomsbury appears to reach out to and touch Clarissa, in the midst of her own party.

From what we know of how the Bloomsbury Group managed their own social lives, the moments of democratic relationship imagined in their fiction belie the class restrictions governing the forms of sociability they generally practised. For Forster, Woolf and the other members of the upper-middle-class cultural clique to which they belonged, the personal connections they forged in Bloomsbury have often been construed as examples of elite social networking within a tightly screened fraction of the local population. One might be led to conclude that the soirées and *conversationes* in which the Bloomsbury Group forged their tight web of interconnected triangular personal relationships were produced despite the contingency of the area's protean social mixture, or even in deliberate contradistinction to it.

Bloomsbury has long been associated with some highly curated kinds of social life and, in some respects, remains so today. However progressive in their aspirations, academia, publishing and the other professions associated with the area operate through the personal introduction, the invitation and other practices that facilitate rigorously selective sociability. Bloomsbury historically acted to enable both kinds of meeting, accidental and contrived. Drawing out the cultural history of one site associated with Bloomsbury's social happenstance – that of the boarding house – this chapter situates two of its culturally significant social networks, the Pre-Raphaelite Brotherhood and the Bloomsbury Group, into this context of the neighbourhood's democratic mingling.

In one very literal sense, Bloomsbury has long facilitated connections between distant parties through the three busy railway stations that face onto its northern border, the Euston Road. The multiple platforms of Euston, built in 1837, King's Cross (1852) and St Pancras (1868), each play host daily to hundreds of emotional scenes of *rendezvous* and *adieux* between family members, friends and lovers. In the nineteenth century, meanwhile, Euston was one of the metropolis's main gateways to the Atlantic, the major port of Liverpool being one of the key destinations for trains leaving north from London. Thus Victorian Bloomsbury functioned as a mediator between different parts of the world just as the locality connected economically divided parts of the city.

Once Eurostar announced its move from Waterloo to St Pancras International, the latter station became an immediate contact zone between Britain and Europe, and Bloomsbury's northern border once more mediates London with the rest of the world. The material value of this re-connection was very quickly legible in changes to the area's built environment, as substantial regeneration money swiftly chased such a major infrastructural investment. Most prominent of all this regeneration activity was the restoration of Gilbert Scott's railway hotel. If asked to demonstrate the persistence of Victorian London within the city we live in today, one could do worse than to begin with the extraordinarily grand Victorian staircase that the five-star

'The Central Hall With Its Models.' Photograph of Euston Station in St John Adcock [ed], *Wonderful London*, 1928. The central statue, created by Carlo Marochetti in 1854, is of railway and civil engineer Robert Stephenson. It now stands in the open forecourt of today's Euston station.

St Pancras Renaissance Hotel has tangibly revived. But, in a sense, this would be missing the more profound way that the station's recent internationalisation recapitulates Bloomsbury's nineteenth-century past. For as node for all kinds of transnational traffic, cultural, social and economic, the new St Pancras International has returned Bloomsbury to its structural role as a district in which the city and the wider world meet.

Partly because of its infrastructural connections to the rest of the world, Bloomsbury has a cosmopolitan feel. Large numbers of visitors from other countries stay there for a few days or months in temporary accommodation. This nomadic quality to the area was true at the beginning of the twentieth century. As Lucas, in 1906, points out, Bloomsbury was the haunt of 'economical Americans', giving 'harbourage to all colours . . . the Baboo law student [being] one of the commonest incidents of its streets.'[2] Nowadays, dotted with enormous hotels and large residential blocks for international students, Bloomsbury hosts a perpetual temporary population of comparative strangers from all over the world thrown together by professional circumstance. Used heavily by organisations and businesses for large residential events, Bloomsbury's industrially scaled bed factories can appear overwhelmingly atomising or alienating. But the more casual or fluid forms of social life that increasingly characterise global modernity flourish here. In this Bloomsbury of international summer schools and conferences, of over-long corridors and identity badges, gregarious intimacies spark continually between people whose paths might otherwise never have crossed.

Whereas today these encounters tend to be staged in dated hotels with dodgy lifts, for most of the nineteenth century and up until the 1940s the locality's boarding houses were key congregation points for unusual social mingling. When they were first built, Bloomsbury's townhouses had been intended

Midland Grand Hotel,

ST. PANCRAS STATION,

LONDON, N.W.

SPECIAL TRAINS RUN BETWEEN ST. PANCRAS STATION AND TILBURY IN CONNECTION WITH THE SAILINGS OF THE

ORIENT LINE
OF
STEAMERS.

ACCOMMODATION AT THE MIDLAND GRAND HOTEL CAN BE WIRED FOR FREE OF CHARGE ON APPLICATION TO THE MIDLAND AGENT AT TILBURY.

FORMS THE LONDON TERMINUS OF THE MIDLAND RAILWAY, WHENCE TRAINS RUN AT CONVENIENT INTERVALS TO ALL PARTS OF

THE NORTH OF ENGLAND AND **SCOTLAND.**

TELEPHONE NO. 502 "KING'S CROSS."

TELEGRAPHIC ADDRESS : "MIDOTEL, LONDON."

New Parisian Restaurant & Ladies' Coffee Room,

EN SUITE WITH THE NEWLY-FURNISHED AND DECORATED WRITING, READING, AND DRAWING ROOMS, IS NOW OPEN FOR THE SERVICE OF HIGH-CLASS FRENCH COOKING AND CHOICE VINTAGE WINES.

The Hotel is very convenient for Ladies and Families and Gentlemen, being within a shilling cab fare of all principal Theatres and City and West End centres.

HEYSHAM TOWER,

near Morecambe

TELEGRAPHIC ADDRESS : " MIDOTEL, HEYSHAM."

TELEPHONE NO. 344 " MORECAMBE."

POSTAL ADDRESS : " HEYSHAM TOWER, NEAR LANCASTER."

A CHARMING WINTER AND SUMMER RESIDENCE.

This Residential Hotel is especially recommended for those requiring a change ; standing in 14 acres of ground, looking over Morecambe Bay. Excellent Golf Links.

Early twentieth-century advertisement for two hotels operated by the Midland Railway. The Midland Grand Hotel at St Pancras, designed by George Gilbert Scott, was open from 1873 to 1935. Much of the original building now forms the St Pancras Renaissance London Hotel, opened in 2011. Heysham Tower, near Morecombe, was run as a hotel by the Midland Railway from 1896 to 1925. It was demolished in the 1980s.

to attract 'the best families' from the upper and upper-middle classes. The area never made the grade, however. In the geographical centre of the metropolis, where the fashion was increasingly to put some distance between one's family home and one's place of work, Bloomsbury was deemed too close for comfort to the City, where so many of London's middle-class men pursued careers.

As a result, the neighbourhood declined in socio-economic terms throughout the nineteenth century. Property values fell steadily in Bloomsbury and, as they did, more and more of its townhouses became split up into multi-occupancy accommodation, classically in the form of boarding houses, which were distinguishable from lodging houses through offering tenants daily meals along with a room.

By the first few decades of the twentieth century, this meant that Bloomsbury was a space that was unusually affordable for central London, making it particularly attractive to international visitors to the city. Full of young people from all around the empire – often studying in the area's academic institutions – the neighbourhood's boarding houses constituted the front line of London's transformation into the fully cosmopolitan world city it is today. For many visitors to the British capital from distant parts of the globe, the burgeoning cosmopolitanism of Bloomsbury's temporary accommodation made it a particularly appealing place to live. C. L. R. James said that a room of an early twentieth-century Bloomsbury lodging house was, on the one hand, 'aesthetically speaking one of the worst places in the world'. On the other hand, it granted the considerable compensation of enabling connections with people to an extent unknown elsewhere in the city or, indeed, the world. 'In Bloomsbury in particular you will meet with all sorts. The intellectuals do not despise the ordinary shop girl and there is not horrible exclusiveness which kills so much of our social life in Trinidad. All that they seem to ask of you is that you be not

'Brunswick Square: Part of Bloomsbury's Boarding-House Land.' Photograph in St John Adcock (ed), *Wonderful London*, 1928.

dull.'[3] The lack of exclusivity that was offered by intellectual cosmopolitan Bloomsbury, meanwhile, acted as a spur to James's own creativity:

> When you lie in bed in the early morning and have not slept and know that you will not sleep because of something you have to do the next day or someone you have to meet . . . these things are the basis of life and of great writing and of great art in any part of the world. You get into contact with them by emotional relationships with people and with things and by communion with your own soul.[4]

Other foreign visitors to Britain, meanwhile, suffered a much less warm sense of welcome on coming into contact with Bloomsbury. Jean Rhys's autobiographical writings *Smile Please* recall her experience of taking rooms 'somewhere in Bloomsbury' when she moved there in the 1930s, straight from Dominica. Colliding with the 'ritual of having a bath in an English boarding-house', she breaks invisible codes that immediately mark her out as a national other or alien, needing to be cleansed not so much physically as culturally:

> On my way to my room I passed the bathroom and thought it would be a good idea to have a bath. I felt not hot, but sticky and a little tired. So I went in and turned the hot tap on. When the bath was half full I undressed and got in, thinking it very pleasant. I began to feel very happy and thought that when the water got cool I would turn the hot tap on again. I began to sing. Then above the noise of the water came a loud voice.
> 'Who's that in there?'
> I answered with my name.
> 'Turn that tap off,' said the voice. 'Turn that tap off at once.'
> I turned it off. All my pleasure had gone and I got out of the bath and into my clothes as quickly as I could. When I reached my room my aunt was waiting for me. I said: 'I'm afraid the landlady is very annoyed with me.'
> 'Of course she's annoyed with you,' said my aunt. 'What possessed you to go into the bathroom and take all the hot water?'[5]

Immigrant communities in Bloomsbury who daily experienced more overt xenophobic or racist hostility could learn to resist it by maintaining a hostile disposition in response. In Julian Maclaren-Ross's *Memoirs from the Forties*, the writer and actor remembers trying to find the Bloomsbury address from which Cyril Connolly's literary magazine *Horizon* operated. Knocking on the wrong door, he discovers instead a community of immigrants, the existence of which he had not been hitherto aware, living almost invisibly alongside the neighbourhood's literary scene:

> [The door] after a stealthy pause came open, a dark face peered cautiously through the crack, then the door was banged-to in my face . . . I climbed higher, knocked, another Indian appeared, small and shrivelled like the first . . . A third occupant, Indian also, seemed to know no English . . . Indians in every flat, either unable or unwilling to give any information, and the last one a woman in a sari shrank in terror when she saw me and almost slammed her door upon my hand.[6]

Dripping as it is in racist anxiety about the 'dark' populations invisibly multiplying in Bloomsbury's multiple occupancy housing, Maclaren-Ross's anecdote is nonetheless clear about the fears or misgivings some ethnic minorities living in the area felt instinctively upon the approach of a white British middle-class stranger. The kinds of 'emotional relationships' across social divides that C. L. R. James attributed to the neighbourhood, it seems, may well have been more rare than his more celebratory account suggests.

By offering plausible scenarios for tense or exuberant inter-cultural encounters, the Bloomsbury boarding house proved a valuable imaginative space for writers, who could dramatise the tensions attending the city's social diversity and yet focus on a confined shared domestic space. Ian Hay's play *Tilly of Bloomsbury* (1919), based on his book *Happy-Go-Lucky* (1913),

"'How do you do, Miss Weller?" said Lady Adela, mystified but well-bred.' Illustration by Charles E. Brock, from Ian Hay, *Happy-Go-Lucky*, Blackwood & Sons 1913. Hay wrote the play version, entitled *Tilly of Bloomsbury*, in 1919.

uses a boarding house around Russell Square in order to hatch and test an unlikely romantic liaison between a landlady's daughter and an aristocrat. Bloomsbury's racial diversity is in evidence in the play. A 'furtive Oriental person' is spotted on the stairs, a 'stout coloured gentleman' whom a character speculates is a student at the London University.[7]

The question of racial difference is marginalised from the main storyline, however, as it explores much more explicitly the theme of class conflict and social mobility. The heroine, Tilly, tries to feign gentility in order to secure the hand in marriage of a man far above her station whom she has met on the top of an omnibus. Pretending that the boarding house run by her mother is her family's freehold property, Tilly recruits her mother, father, sister and all the lodgers to act the part of wealthy friends and relatives, until the farcical situation inevitably breaks down and she is forced to confess:

> TILLY.   Mother keeps lodgings. This house is a lodging house, and those men you saw just now are two of the lodgers. Percy [her brother] serves behind the counter in a haberdasher's shop in Holborn. I do a little dress designing. Little 'Melia waits on the lodgers. You see, you have been done! We work for a living.[8]

Tilly of Bloomsbury was filmed in 1921, 1931 and 1940. The story's success on the big screen depended on its happy ending, in which 'mutual love' triumphs over class prejudice. Dick, the aristocrat, proposes marriage, despite her conniving behaviour and social inferiority:

> DICK.   I believe in mutual love; I believe that kind hearts are more than coronets; I believe that a merry heart goes all the way; and I believe that no difficulty matters a cent so long as you can face it in the right company. That is what you and I are going to do – face this old world, with its joys and sorrows, in one another's company.[9]

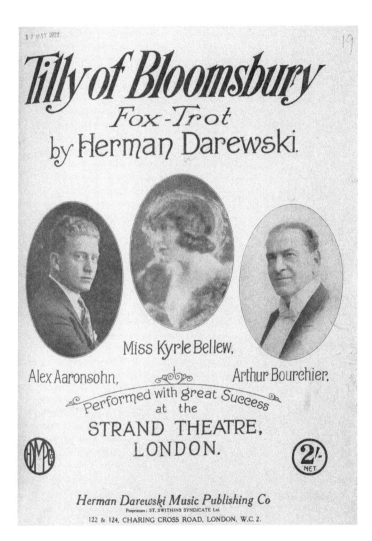

Titlepage in book of sheet music for the play *Tilly of Bloomsbury*. Herman Dareweski, Music Publishing Co., *c.* 1921.

George Cruickshank, illustration for 'The Boarding House' in Charles Dickens, *Sketches by Boz*, Chapman & Hall, 1839.

George Cruickshank, illustration for 'The Boarding House', in Charles Dickens, *Sketches by Boz*, Chapman & Hall, 1839.

As the long-lived success of *Tilly of Bloomsbury* insists, the area's association in the cultural imagination with the kind of accidental incongruous connection produced by its socially mixed boarding houses survived long after the area had also become identified with the much more exclusive kinds of sociability pertaining to the Bloomsbury Group.

Long before Hay's play and the subsequent films, Bloomsbury's boarding houses had proved extremely useful settings for writers to tell stories about encounter and connection between strangers of different social class. Virtually Charles Dickens's first ever piece of fiction, 'The Boarding House' (1834), sets its comic tale of precarious class identity and sexual frisson in temporary accommodation in Great Coram Street. Anthony Trollope uses Burton Crescent for the boarding-house scenes in *The Small House at Allington* (1864), in which the hapless hero Johnny Eames gets problematically entangled in a relationship with the Cockney landlady's daughter, when he should be concentrating entirely on Lily Dale. George Gissing, meanwhile, borrows the cheap digs in Gower Place he had himself taken only a couple of years previously for his first novel, *Workers in the Dawn* (1880), in which an aspirational young man tries and fails to resist being contaminated by the shabby manners of his inmates there. All of these texts use the Bloomsbury boarding house as a means to explore the sexual opportunities and dangers of strangers with different origins living in close proximity to one another.

Margaret Oliphant's *A House in Bloomsbury* (1894) anatomises quite explicitly the hierarchies at work in a boarding house situated at the corner of a street near Russell Square. In the opening chapters, the heroine takes the reader around the establishment, allowing the narrator to present it as a kind of microcosm for society, a microcosm in which social distinction is indexed vertically and connected by means of the shared stairs. Here she ascends to the top of the house, to introduce us to the poorest of the tenants:

Dora ran up the stairs, which were dark at the top, for [the landlady] could not afford to let her lodgers who paid so low a rent have a light on their landing; and the landing itself was encumbered by various articles, between which there was need of wary steering. But this little girl had lived in these Bloomsbury lodgings all her life, and knew her way about as well as the children of the house.[10]

A chapter or so later, our heroine fills in some of the gaps, including not only the richest of the tenants in her itinerary but also the lower-class boarding-house keeper herself, a character type of the genre of Bloomsbury boarding-house fiction that plays a key role in Dickens's, Trollope's and Gissing's earlier texts:

Dora was free of the whole house, and . . . she used her *petites entrées* in the most liberal and democratic fashion, thinking no scorn of going downstairs sometimes to the funny little room next to the kitchen, which [the landlady] called the breakfast-room, and used as her own sanctum, the family centre where her grandchildren and herself found refuge out of the toils of the kitchen . . . It is not often that a young person in search of the entertainment of sympathy has all the gradations of the social system to choose from. The first floor represented the aristocracy in the establishment at Bloomsbury . . . When the girl felt that her needs required the sympathy of a person of the highest, *i.e.*, her own class, she went either boldly or with strategy to the drawing-room floor.[11]

Contriving '*petites entrées*' between characters occupying not only different floors of the house but also 'all the gradations of the social system', Bloomsbury boarding-house fiction exploits the social, and often sexual, tension that inevitably arises from multiple bodies mingling accidentally in one domestic space. As Oliphant's word 'democratic' suggests, there is a political dimension to these stories of circumstantial encounter. For conservative writers such as Oliphant, these meetings between characters from different class backgrounds often begin with 'sympathy' but tend towards vice or crime, thus articulating an anxiety about modern democracy.

Thrusting together people from different classes and ethnicities, Bloomsbury's boarding houses were crucibles of modernity by virtue of the kinds of social connections they produced by accident. Neighbouring addresses on the same streets and squares, comprising more conventional residential compositions, also fostered modern forms of sociability, doing so intentionally and not as a by-product of business. In the nineteenth and twentieth centuries, two of the most identifiable cliques within British cultural history formed in Bloomsbury's townhouses – the Pre-Raphaelite Brotherhood and the Bloomsbury Group. Both of these groups had a strong sense of their separateness from the broader culture in which they found themselves, yet each also engaged in complex ways with the socially diverse neighbourhood with which they were identified. These groups were founded and sustained by social occasions that were far from accidental. Yet both of these 'invite only' cliques, which were formed in Bloomsbury, drew energy from the messier social milieu of the neighbourhood.

A family townhouse on Gower Street sets the scene for the foundation in 1848 of the first of Britain's artistic self-conscious groupings. The Pre-Raphaelite Brotherhood's lead member John Millais was the youngest ever member of the Royal Academy when he was admitted there at the age of eleven. His prior training was rooted in Bloomsbury, the young prodigy having sketched the statues in the British Museum almost as soon as he could draw. The seeds of the PRB were sown when Millais offered his friend and colleague William Holman Hunt the use of his studio. Sitting up all night, the pair strained to finish their respective paintings for the imminent Royal Academy annual competition. Working together allowed them to 'encourage each other and talk over [their] ambitions'. An

William Holman Hunt, *John Everett Millais*. Pencil portrait of Millais aged twenty-four. 1853.

intense friendship based on mutual personal attachment and non-competitive professional endeavour blossomed out of these nocturnal meetings:

> It was from these evening stances, and the confidence engendered by the free interchange of thought, that sprang the determination of these youths to leave the beaten track of art and strike out a new line for themselves. Raphael, the idol of the art world, they dared to think, was not altogether free from imperfections ... They must go back to earlier times for examples of sound and satisfactory work, and, rejecting the teaching of the day that blindly followed in his footsteps, must take Nature as their only guide. They would go to her, and her alone, for inspiration; and, hoping that others would be tempted to join in their crusade against conventionality, they selected as their distinctive title the term 'Pre-Raphaelites'.[12]

That initial friendship between Millais and Hunt may have provided the ground work for the emergence of the PRB, but it was their mutual friend Dante Gabriel Rossetti who pursued most vigorously the possibility of forming a distinct artistic group. Gathering the seven members who comprised its initial instantiation, Rossetti's gregarious desire to expand the group appears to have been countered by a 'jealous' impulse on the part of Millais and Hunt to restrict the membership of what he himself named a 'clique':

> The first meeting, at which terms of co-operation were seriously discussed, was held on a certain night in 1848, at Millais' home in Gower Street, where the young artist exhibited, as examples of sound work, some volumes of engravings from the frescoes of Benozzo Gozzoli, Orcagua, and others now in the Campo Santo at Pisa. 'Now, look here', said Millais, speaking for himself and Hunt, who were both jealous of others joining them without a distinct understanding of their object, 'this is what the Pre-Raphaelite clique should follow'. The idea was eagerly taken up, and then, or shortly afterwards, William Rossetti, Woolner,

F. G. Stephens (now an Art critic), and James Collinson joined the Brotherhood . . . [13]

At the same time as maintaining a strong sense of the exclusivity of their cooperative endeavour, many members of the PRB reached out in various ways to the working-class population of Bloomsbury. Millais and Hunt had, in 1848, joined the largest ever Chartist demonstration, a march dedicated to the political enfranchisement of the working classes that began in Russell Square and ended in Kennington Common. Many of the Pre-Raphaelites were, moreover, linked with Christian socialism, a liberal theological movement from this period that argued that the Church's chief mission was to address the 'great gulf fixed' between the poor and the rich.

Christian socialism was heavily associated with Bloomsbury. One of its key figures, F. D. Maurice, founded his Working Men's College there, in Great Ormond Street, in 1854. Maurice thought that the example of Christ suggested that the inequalities of the nineteenth century could be ameliorated through cross-class fellowship and cooperation, and he set up his college in order to foster such meetings across the divide of economic inequality. Many members of the original Brotherhood, including Rossetti, taught there, as did later members Edward Burne-Jones and William Morris (who had moved to Great Ormond Street in 1856 after his undergraduate days at Oxford). In Victorian Bloomsbury boarding-house fiction, cross-class relations were a source of tension that writers exploited for a range of effects, both comic and tragic. By having played such an important role in this project of cross-class social connection, the 'clique' of the Pre-Raphaelite Brotherhood can be seen to have engaged with the contingency of Bloomsbury's social mixture.

That network of intellectuals and artists of the twentieth century known as the Bloomsbury Group was also very much a product of the neighbourhood, and needs to be understood in relation to the unusual social mixture of its population. From

View of the Working Men's College, Great Ormond Street, in John Llewelyn Davies, *The Working Men's College 1854-1904: Records of its History and Work for Fifty Years*, Macmillan & Co., 1904.

Houses in Gordon Square, including No.46, home to Virginia, Vanessa, Adrian and Thoby Stephen from 1904 to 1907.

Photographic portrait of Virginia Woolf, by George Charles Beresford, 1902.

1904, when the Stephen siblings (two of whom became better known as Vanessa Bell and Virginia Woolf) moved to the area from West London after their father died, they identified strongly with its pre-existing bohemianism, contrasting 'free' Bloomsbury with the stuffy conservatism of the area from which they had come. This bohemianism was largely produced by the boarding houses, as spaces that thrust together young single people who were liberated from the strictures of the communities of their origins, be they rich or poor, metropolitan or colonial. On an everyday level, many of the Bloomsbury Group were elitist and snobbish in their interactions with the working class, but on a symbolic level, the preference of Woolf and the others for Bloomsbury over Kensington signals a deep desire to be affiliated with the democratic social mixture that the West Central district harboured.

The painters Vanessa Bell, Roger Fry and Duncan Grant, the economist John Maynard Keynes, and the writers Virginia Woolf and Lytton Strachey, all made important interventions into their respective fields of intellectual endeavour. Considered together they constitute the single most influential alliance to feature in the British cultural scene before the Second World War. Still, while they shared much philosophical and political ground, the experiments in personal and sexual life they made together in Bloomsbury's townhouses arguably made as important an impact upon the wider culture as their intellectual or artistic collaborations. As Woolf recognises in her memoirs, the Group's sexual dissidence was one of their most important contributions to 'civilisation'. Her recollection underlines the fact that this collective contribution belonged to Bloomsbury and, implicitly, could not have happened elsewhere:

> So there was nothing that one could not say, nothing that one could not do, at 46 Gordon Square. It was, I think, a great advance in civilisation. It may be true that the loves of buggers are not – at least if one is of the other persuasion – of enthralling or paramount importance.

But the fact that they can be mentioned openly leads to the fact no one minds if they are practised privately. Thus many customs and beliefs were revised. Indeed the future of Bloomsbury was to prove that many variations can be played on the theme of sex . . .[14]

All of these 'variations upon sex' took place within a series of socially interconnected Bloomsbury houses, starting with 46 Gordon Square, the home of Virginia, Vanessa, Adrian and Thoby Stephen from 1904 to 1907. It was there that they hosted their 'Thursday evenings', informal weekly parties that were attended by Thoby's Cambridge friends. When Vanessa and Clive Bell remained together there after the pair married, the 'open house' conviviality that had been established when they were all single continued. From 1911 to 1912, Virginia and Adrian shared 38 Brunswick Square with Grant, Keynes and Leonard Woolf – the two Bloomsbury households loved in triangles and lived in each other's pockets. A whole host of other Bloomsbury addresses continued to participate in this important 'revision' of culture, an intervention that helped to change attitudes towards not only homosexuality, but also heterosociality (mutual non-sexual friendship between men and women).

It is hard not to fault the Bloomsbury Group for their exclusivity. The everyday social snobbishness that circulated within this tight circle of friends clearly compromised the liberal, internationalist, anti-colonial politics that many of them espoused. But, reading between the lines of Woolf's recollection of their sexual dissidence, it is possible to see that she saw their exclusiveness as a precondition for the sexual candour of the Group. For the 'open house' polyamory that flourished in the Bloomsbury Group at the beginning of the twentieth century was clearly dependent, paradoxically, upon a cautious door policy. The 'loves of buggers' were, after all, a matter of 'paramount importance' that was sufficient for some reactionary judges to justify sending convicted homosexuals standardly to jail. Some sort of filter would have to be applied to those legendary Bloomsbury parties in order to stop anyone from ruining everybody's fun.

Nonetheless, the snobbishness and racism that evidently circulated within the ostensibly socially liberal world of the Bloomsbury Group cannot be excused in the light of their collective contributions of the history of sexuality in the way one used to excuse the bad behaviour of individual geniuses in the light of the beautiful poems they produced. In approaching cultural history, thankfully, we don't have to act as judge, jury or executioner. We can instead consider the Bloomsbury Group's relationship to Bloomsbury social life more dispassionately.

Removing the railings in Russell Square, 17 November 1941.

Chapter 4   **Railing**

In 1944, British Pathé released a documentary entitled *Out and About*, which contained a three-minute sequence recommending Bloomsbury as a tourist destination.[1] Glorying in its elegant Georgian architecture, the townhouses of Bedford Square and other well-to-do Bloomsbury addresses are contrasted favourably with the modernist skyscraper of Senate House which overshadows them. At first glance, the film seems designed simply to reassure war-weary viewers that much of old London had survived the Blitz, just as they themselves had. Beyond this straightforward imperative, however, there is also something subversive in the film, which can be discerned in its oddly excessive focus on the area's railings.

'When you're out and about in London, you're bound to be reminded – especially in Bloomsbury – of its association with Charles Dickens, but there are modern curiosities as well . . .' Thus begins the chirpy RP middle-aged male voiceover, drawing viewers into what at first seems like a straightforward account of the cultural heritage of one of the world's most famous literary localities. Almost immediately, however, we veer away from a standard roll call of sites to visit, and are granted instead a series of images of contemporary Bloomsbury whose selection is curious indeed, consisting as it does largely of shots of the area's ironwork. Throughout the short film, the juxtaposition of camerawork and voiceover works obliquely to raise questions about the politics of railings, those ubiquitous and usually unremarked features of the London streetscape.

The text of the voiceover, which continually shuttles between Bloomsbury's genteel Georgian past and the wartime present, marks the change between these moments in history by linking the proliferation of industrial metalwork in the area with its economic decline: 'London's central district was once its wealthiest, but the glitter of gold has since given way to another Iron Age, with railings of infinite variety, some of them beautifully spiked.' To exemplify the aesthetic quality of what might otherwise be discounted as merely functional street furniture, a shot of attractive wrought iron railings follows. This is undercut, however, by the next shot, which shows us some unattractive barbed wire topping a wall – a utilitarian domestic security feature that feels out of place in a cinematic tourism advertisement, and which is in any case beyond the purview of the tourist on foot. The script continues by gesturing to the unequal property distribution that underwrites the prevalence of such variably attractive spiky objects in the neighbourhood: 'The railings and the spikes help to protect the Ducal property. These same railings encompass Bloomsbury's many squares, of which Russell, Bedford and Bloomsbury are perhaps the best known.' Alongside the voiceover's nudge to the aristocratic habit of stamping the family names upon the family land, the camera bears witness to a woman carrying a child in her arms slowly walking on the pavement around Bedford Square, a garden oasis from which she is implicitly excluded.

From this point on, the documentary becomes quietly more insistent upon the contemporary politics of the locality's railings. Even as the voiceover places the 'gardens and houses' of Bloomsbury in an obsolescent 'Old World', we are shown footage of the railings surrounding these aristocratic spaces being cheerfully removed by workmen. These shots, of course, document a much publicised component of the domestic war effort, when the ironwork around London's private garden squares was commandeered by the military for its apparent redeployment in airplanes, tanks or ammunitions. Images of active young modern-looking men with goggles cutting

Railings and a locked gate, Bedford Square, April 2017.

through the spikes accompany the voiceover's 'spiky' prose: 'The iron age of Bloomsbury has yielded in turn to the demands of war – the iron that decorated is now becoming the iron that destroys.' Throughout the film, the closing shot of which is of the iron gates to the British Museum slowly shutting, the railings are implicitly treated as part of an exclusionary anachronistic world that is being actively dismantled.

Following D-Day, as the war on the Home Front wound down, the question about what to do about London's railings was becoming implicated in much larger questions about what kind of peace lay ahead for working-class Londoners. In parts of the city such as Bloomsbury, which in the middle of the twentieth century housed large populations of poorer Londoners with little access to the many garden squares in their midst, the mooted return of the removed railings represented a retrograde step and a threat to the more egalitarian future they had fought so hard to secure. The war with Nazi Germany may have been ending, but the railings reminded viewers of a class struggle that was still ongoing. Between the lines of its interposed imagery and commentary, the Bloomsbury episode of *Out and About* suggests that the beautiful spikes it ostensibly celebrates might be a part of the past unworthy of being preserved.

In the same year the film was released, George Orwell wrote an article for left-wing newspaper *Tribune* that decries much more explicitly the anti-democratic politics of the railings:

> I see that the railings are returning – only wooden ones, it is true, but still railings – in one London square after another. So the lawful denizens of the squares can make use of their treasured keys again, and the children of the poor can be kept out.
>
> When the railings round the parks and squares were removed, the object was partly to accumulate scrap-iron, but the removal was also felt to be a democratic gesture. Many more green spaces were now open to the public, and you could stay in the parks till all hours instead of being hounded out at closing times by grim-faced keepers. It was also discovered that these railings were not only unnecessary

but hideously ugly. The parks were improved out of recognition by being laid open, acquiring a friendly, almost rural look that they had never had before. And had the railings vanished permanently, another improvement would probably have followed. The dreary shrubberies of laurel and privet – plants not suited to England and always dusty, at any rate in London – would probably have been grubbed up and replaced by flower beds. Like the railings, they were merely put there to keep the populace out. However, the higher-ups managed to avert this reform, like so many others, and everywhere the wooden palisades are going up, regardless of the wastage of labour and timber.[2]

Just like the contemporaneous Pathé footage, Orwell's response to the gradual return of the railings highlights the physical materials from which these elements of street furniture are made. In the passage above he notes warily the insidious replacement of 'hideously ugly' cast iron with makeshift 'palisades' of timber, pointing to the waste of valuable wood that could be more valuably directed to the repair of bomb-damaged buildings.

Recently, the artist Catalina Pollak Williamson exploited the material resonances of railings made specifically of cast iron when she commemorated the 'democratic gesture' of their removal in the Second World War. Installed throughout the summer of 2012 in Malet Place, her imaginative sound art piece *Phantom Railings* ambushed pedestrians with sounds resembling those of a wooden stick run against iron bars. Keeping pace with anyone passing along the pavement, these surprising sounds were emitted in response to movement sensors concealed amidst the stumps of railings that once surrounded the Sunken Gardens, a green space owned by the university that is now open only intermittently to the general public. Educating thousands of Bloomsbury's pedestrians about the important moment that precipitated the transfer of most of its private squares into public ownership, the installation arrested its audience's attention aurally, teasing out the invisible politics of objects that tend to go unnoticed even when they are physically present.

That sound of a stick run upon iron railings ingeniously conjured the spectre of forgotten scenes of everyday resistance by citizens like Orwell, who had in the past *railed against* the exclusion and division that characterised the privatised city before the war. Through the embodied experience it enacted, *Phantom Railings* reminded twenty-first-century pedestrians of a historical struggle that was fought in Bloomsbury and elsewhere for the democratisation of London's open space. While railings act materially as bulwarks to sustain the status quo, by contrast to 'rail against' means to resist and demonstrate, to protest and try to effect change. The objects of railings and the action of railing against both point us to a power struggle, but from different sides of the fence, so to speak.

This tension within, or flexibility of, the word 'railing', is particularly well suited to having been staged in Bloomsbury. The iron street furniture that Orwell called ugly is today one of Bloomsbury's most prized features, after all. Maintaining an aesthetic continuity with a pre-democratic past, the recently restored railings that now enclose Gordon Square or Russell Square are bathed in the nostalgic glow that the heritage industry increasingly draws upon to commodify London for tourism and real estate. But Bloomsbury is also a place that has been persistently defined by resistance and rebellion, a place defined by the railings and rantings of individuals and groups who have refused in one way or another to submit to the unyielding metal of the powerful or wealthy. Having fostered various forms of radicalism and political dissent, Bloomsbury has been at least as much associated with railings against power than with the power embodied by railings themselves.

On more than one occasion, Bloomsbury's railings have themselves become appropriated physically in the cause of political dissent. In 1815, for instance, they were torn down and used as weapons in the protests that railed against the passing of the Corn Laws, legislative Acts which protected landowners' interests at the expense of urban working-class consumers.

Railings around the British Museum, April 2017.

But an even more subversive use of railings – and certainly the most famous – was that performed by the suffragettes, a group associated with Bloomsbury who chained themselves to iron bars repeatedly in order to draw attention to the injustice of denying women the vote. These manoeuvres, in which railings are themselves used unexpectedly as a means to fight back against the status quo, appear to belong, peculiarly, to Bloomsbury, a district whose aristocratic pedigree is branded into every street and square, and yet which also played a major role in the history of socialism, anti-colonialism and feminism.

Long before Orwell, railings in Bloomsbury had become embroiled in a left-wing political discussion about the rights of London's working-class citizens to its open space. In 1874, the private squares of the Bedford estate were made subject to controversy in the press, the radical *Preston Guardian* arguing strongly against Bloomsbury's railings and insisting that the Duke's gardens be opened up to the public: 'now it is announced, on the very best authority, that His Grace the Duke of Bedford has promised to re-arrange, replant, and otherwise beautify Bedford-square. I can only hope that the Duke will be advised to take down the railings and throw open the square honestly and entirely open.'[3]

The middle-class *Graphic* thought this idea several steps too far, and hinted that the idea had a worryingly French air about it:

A London square is totally different to a Continental place, and Londoners choose squares to live in simply because they are quieter than streets. It is rather hard if a person who rents a house in a square for the sake of quiet suddenly finds the enclosure turned into a public garden, for after all there is nothing more annoying to the ears than the hum of multitudes and the crooning of children . . . It may be imagined that the inhabitants of . . . Bedford, Russell, and Fitzroy – would scarcely view a project for their annexation to the public parks with any violent demonstrations of delight. Public gardens are excellent things, but private rights certainly merit a little consideration.[4]

The lexicon of this passage reveals the broader anxieties lurking behind its author's disinterested tone, and the easy slippage from the 'hum of the multitudes' to 'violent demonstrations' is surely not coincidental. In 1866, the Reform League had marched to Hyde Park to protest for an enlargement of the franchise, and had gone against police diktat by breaking down the railings to gain entrance to their destination. Even more recently, and more worryingly, the Communards had torn down railings to form the barricades in Paris. Rather than the author's ostensible concern that his quiet afternoons might be disturbed by the 'crooning of children', the deeper fear might well be that the absence of railings might encourage new forms of public gathering that could lead to the construction of a more equal form of society.

In her artwork *Phantom Railings*, Pollak Williamson echoed a moment in the utopian romance *News from Nowhere* (1890) by the most famous British socialist of the nineteenth century, William Morris. Hundreds of years after a revolution has radically changed society for the better, the narrator, who has time-travelled from the late nineteenth century, discovers that the British Museum is a very rare architectural survival from the pre-revolutionary world he recognises: 'We walked straight into the forecourt of the Museum, where, except that the railings were gone, and the whispering boughs of the trees were all about, nothing seemed changed; the very pigeons were wheeling about the building and clinging to the ornaments of the pediment as I had seen them of old.'[5]

That Morris keeps the museum within his utopia, but very deliberately removes the railings that surround them, makes as clear a point about the reactionary politics of these items of Bloomsbury's street furniture as Pollack Williamson's sound art has done much more recently.

Bloomsbury's railings were brought directly into arguments made by socialists such as Morris and Orwell about unequal access to space in the capitalist city. But Bloomsbury was a part of London that was concerned with contestations over space on a much more global scale too. Largely because of its universities, hosting students from all over the British Empire, in the first half of the twentieth century Bloomsbury became heavily associated with the anti-colonial movement. The School of Oriental and African Studies, better known as SOAS, still has a reputation for being one of the most radical campuses in this respect, both in terms of the critical slant of its teaching of history and international relations, and in the substantial involvement of its student body in anti-racism and anti-war activism. The heyday of Bloomsbury as a site for railing against imperialism, however, was the first few decades of the twentieth century.

In C. L. R. James's recollection, the area acted in the 1930s as a seedbed of anti-colonial discourse between committed young people from all corners of the British Empire, who would share ideas with each other about how best to overthrow the colonial yoke. Conversation there moved standardly from discussions about 'D. H. Lawrence, Bolshevik Russia, [and] sex' to 'the Indian question, British Imperialism, Abyssinia, [and] coloured students in London'.[6] James's account attests to the thrilling, exhausting schedule of events that constituted the anti-colonial Bloomsbury that he experienced as a student:

> I delivered the lecture that night to the Society of International Studies. In the very same building Mr C. F. Andrews was speaking to another society interested in Indian Nationalism and people from his meeting kept on coming into mine. The lecture was fairly successful because after it was finished I received two invitations – one to join the Friends of India Society, which meets on the first Monday of every month, and the other to lecture on any subject connected with the West Indies at the Indian Students' Central Association. You might think that was enough for one day. You simply do not know Bloomsbury.[7]

Bloomsbury was particularly significant for its association with the cause of Indian independence, a fact still marked by the statues of Gandhi in Tavistock Square and Rabindranath Tagore in

Mahatma Gandhi, sculpted by Fredda Brilliant and installed in Tavistock Gardens in 1968. The pedestal was deliberately made hollow for people to leave floral tributes to Gandhi.

Bust of Rabindranath Tagore, by Shenda Armery, in Gordon Square. The bust of the Nobel prizewinner was unveiled in 2011, on the six-year anniversary of the 7 July bombing nearby at Tavistock Square.

Gordon Square. Gandhi and Tagore were two of a cohort of Indian students who in the later nineteenth century increasingly came to study law at University College (it was a relatively accessible institution for non-Christians because it was avowedly non-denominational). The Indian Students' Union and Hostel opened in 1920, in the 'Shakespeare Hut' on the corner of Keppel Street and Gower Street, as a branch of the YMCA catering to south Asians studying in London. Moving to 106–112 Gower Street in 1923, these premises not only residentially accommodated individuals new to the metropole, but also convened a series of important anti-colonial talks and lectures, by figures including Gandhi and Nehru. A bomb in the Battle of Britain destroyed the building, killing one student, following which tragedy the hostel moved addresses until it found its current home in 41 Fitzroy Square in 1950. This venue was opened by Krishna Menon, a figure who lived in various lodgings in Bloomsbury before moving just north of the area. As the leader of the Indian League, which actively campaigned for Indian self-government, but also serving as a Labour Party councillor for the predominantly working-class ward of St Pancras from 1934 to 1947, Menon railed against political injustices on both a local and a global scale.

On occasion, Bloomsbury enabled the radicalisation of colonial subjects not so much through the way it facilitated meetings between fellow sub-alterns but, ironically, by the way it put them into contact with the arrogance of the British literary establishment. In *Conversations in Bloomsbury*, Mulk Raj Anand recalls some prickly dialogue between D. H. Lawrence, T. S. Eliot, Aldous Huxley and himself in a Bloomsbury bookshop, the racist undertones of which confirmed his determination to join the fight against his colonial oppressors:

> While I helped to clean the glasses, I realised that I had taken umbrage about wrong words said about India, and for being considered 'lesser breeds beyond the law'. The humiliation for being inferior seemed like a wound in my soul, which would never heal. The more I licked

it the more it became tender. And I decided in my mind that I would fight for the freedom of my country forever, though I may admire these English writers for their literary skills. The thing that disturbed me was that I might get a scholarship from the Silver Wedding Fund of King George and Queen Mary, which my Professor in University College had recommended me for. And then I would be a hypocrite, hating British rule in India and living on its dole.[8]

Just as Bloomsbury's educational institutions afforded colonial subjects opportunities to plan the overthrow of the British Empire, likewise the pioneering access they granted women meant that the neighbourhood became a stage for the feminist cause. Most significant in the history of women's academic emancipation was University College London, which became in 1878 the first university in the country to admit women on the same terms as men. However, the spirit of radical gender innovation in education had been a feature of the area for decades before then. The very first female higher education institution in the country was Bedford College, based in Bedford Square from its opening in 1849 to 1874, when it moved to larger premises out of Bloomsbury. In addition to a specialist ladies' college for medicine, which opened in 1876 in Handel Street, Bloomsbury also hosted a pioneering bi-gendered arts college – the Slade School for Art at UCL – that catered to both men and women from the time that it opened in 1871.

While all of these institutions had a restrictedly middle- and upper-class clientele, Bloomsbury was also the location of a significant educational facility for poor women. The Working Women's College opened in Queen Square in 1864, less than a decade after its brother organisation had been established by F. D. Maurice. More practical, vocational education than one would receive at the university or Bedford College was offered by the Society for Promoting the Employment of Women (SPEW), which opened in 1860, also in Queen Square, and taught women the rudiments of accountancy, law-writing and book-keeping. Residential institutions, meanwhile, allowed middle-class women

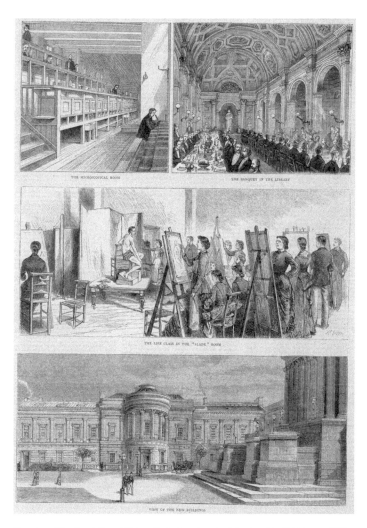

'Opening of the New Wing of University College, London.' *The Graphic*, 26 February 1881.
In the centre, 'The Life Class in the "Slade" Room' depicts students working in the new
space alloted to this pioneering art school, founded at UCL in 1871.

the opportunity to live near their place of study or work. The Home for Lady Arts Students, in Brunswick Square, opened in 1879, while the Ladies' Residential Chambers in Chenies Street provided single-sex accommodation for professional women from 1889. As feminist campaigner Emily Hobhouse says categorically in 1900: 'Bloomsbury is the beloved, the chosen for working women'.[9]

Before the establishment of any of these institutions, however, Bloomsbury had played a significant role in the history of feminism and in the fight for gender equality. It was while living in Store Street, in 1791–92, that Mary Wollstonecraft wrote *A Vindication of the Rights of Women*. One of the founding texts of feminist theory, the *Vindication* responded to deficiencies or blind-spots within the progressive agenda that had been opened up by male democrats such as Thomas Paine, in the immediate aftermath of the 'events in France' of 1789. Arguing for education and employment for women, as well as for the recalibration of the institution of marriage towards mutual companionship between the sexes, Wollstonecraft's treatise has been an inspiration to generations of feminists ever since. Another Bloomsbury feminist, South African novelist Olive Schreiner, paid homage to her intellectual ancestor when she wrote an introduction to a new edition of Wollstonecraft's *Vindications*. When she first came to England in 1882, Schreiner moved to 116 Guilford Street, and in Bloomsbury participated in a network of friendship with other female writers, all of whom worked in the British Museum reading room.

Several works of fiction from the latter part of the nineteenth century construct the area as a space defined by the struggle for women's independence. Isabella Ford's *On the Threshold* (1895) depicts Bloomsbury streets brimming with political potential, both for feminist and socialist causes. At the beginning of the novel, students Lucretia Bampfylde and Kitty Manners move into cheap digs together in Bloomsbury. Bidding for female autonomy and solidarity, these friends self-consciously exchange bourgeois

'Mary Wollstonecraft Godwin.' Frontispiece portrait in Mary Wollstonecraft, *Vindication of the Rights of Women*, from an edition published in 1798.

comfort for bohemian freedom, and their cheerful toleration of the less than salubrious environment of a typical Bloomsbury boarding house clearly emblematises their willingness to engage with, rather than escape from, social reality. The dingy old-fashioned interior of the house in Bloomsbury was celebrated as the grounds for a rejection of parental tyranny:

> The hard, stiff sofa, the hideous sideboard, the one comfortable chair, comfortable only because the bottom was gradually bursting out, seemed like enchanted furniture out of fairy-land, the fairy-land of freedom, where no authoritative and disapproving eye was perpetually on us.
>
> The view from the window on to a macadamised road, with dingy houses opposite, each exactly alike – a road perpetually blocked with heaps of sharp stones and a snorting, road-mending engine – was like the outlook from the windows of a house in Paradise, and the engine was like a band of silver trumpets blowing triumphant hymns to Liberty.[10]

Ford's narrator, Lucretia, imagines the 'snorting, road-mending engine' as the 'triumphant' vanguard liberating a city after a siege, an image that anticipates Bloomsbury's connection not only with the movement towards a fuller 'freedom' for women but also with militancy in that movement. Towards the end of the nineteenth century and at the beginning of the twentieth, Bloomsbury became heavily associated with the suffragettes, who took direct action, in multiple forms, including hunger strikes and, significantly, political martyrdom. Many of the key figures involved in the campaign for votes for women, both militants and non-militants, lived or worked in the area, Millicent Garrett Fawcett and Emmeline Pankhurst among them.

Fawcett, a founder member of the London Society for Women's Suffrage in 1867, lived at No. 2 Gower Street, while Pankhurst lived in Russell Square in the 1890s, hosting parties at which feminists mingled with and learnt tactics from other radical figures, including anarchists such as Peter Kropotkin. Up until 1903, when

Emmeline and Christabel Pankhurst on the roof terrace of their apartment in Clements Inn, Chancery Lan , to the south of Bloomsbury. This was also the home of the WSPU (the Women's Social and Political Union), founded by Christabel in 1903.

Pankhurst founded the Women's Social and Political Union, Fawcett and the Pankhursts had worked together in the cause of women's suffrage, but Fawcett disagreed with the militant tactics of the WSPU and founded the Women's Freedom League as an alternative. Bloomsbury can be seen thus as the grounds within which debates within feminism about how best to rail against the political oppression of women were staged.

While the institutions and houses of Bloomsbury provided platforms for feminists to network and debate, its streets also played host to one of the most visible signs of popular support for the suffragette cause. The memorial service of UCL graduate Emily Davison, who died after throwing herself under the King's horse at the 1913 Epsom Derby, was held at St George's, Bloomsbury. One of the most important events of the suffragette movement, 50,000 people lined the streets to watch her oak coffin make its way up to King's Cross station, after which it was transported to Davison's home town of Morpeth, Northumberland. The service itself was a relatively short affair, but the grand procession which preceded and followed it was a completely extraordinary political event, the like of which Bloomsbury had never seen before. The funeral carriage was pulled by four black horses, alongside which marched six of the most prominent suffragettes, followed by some fifty hunger strikers and hundreds of women ex-prisoners.

Davison's grave in Northumberland was marked with a monument saying 'Deeds not Words', one of the mottos of the suffragette movement, encapsulating their conviction that in order to rail successfully against the patriarchy one would need to take direct action, such as chaining oneself to railings, in order to achieve it. The motto pays homage to the sacrificial act Davison herself made for the political liberation of future women, but it might also be thought of in relation to the funeral procession too. The event was, after all, itself a remarkable collective political deed. The photographs of enormous crowds on either side of Bloomsbury's pavements that appeared in the press would have made a stronger argument than anything said at the funeral service.

Crowds line the street at the funeral procession of Emily Davison, 14 June 1913.

A letter printed in *The Times* on the day of the funeral, on behalf of the Commissioner of Police to Mary Allen of the WSPU, indicates that the authorities were nervous about the potential enormity of the procession's turnout, and tried to suggest an alternative route:

> Madam, – Having regard to the traffic conditions in the streets through which the funeral procession has to pass, I am directed to warn you that as all reasonable facilities must be given to the ordinary traffic, the progress of the proposed funeral *cortège* may be greatly hindered, and if the crowd of sightseers is more than usually large it may prove impracticable for the hearse to reach the church in time for the service there.
>
> In order to convey the remains from one railway station to another in a seemly and reverent manner, the hearse should be accompanied by a limited number of mourners only and taken through streets where traffic conditions will not interfere with its progress. The police will be prepared to indicate a suitable route. – I am, madam, your obedient servant.
>
> W. H. KENDALL, Chief Clerk.[11]

Though Kendall feigns a duty of care to the WSPU, worrying on their behalf that the 'reverence' of the transportation of Davison's remains might be jeopardised by a large crowd of sightseers, his missive reads now as a disingenuous attempt to warn those 'sightseers' off, or even to encourage the 'ordinary traffic' to feel aggrieved at the temporary disruption of their streets. The suffragettes ignored police advice and stuck to their proposed route, which went through the whole of central London, from Victoria to Bloomsbury, gathering crowds by accretion until the final, intentionally slowed down, leg of the journey from the church to the railway station.

In Ford's *On the Threshold*, a young woman imagines the streets of London appropriated for the cause of emancipation, 'a band of silver trumpets blowing triumphant hymns to Liberty'. In a strange way, Davison's funeral momentarily put such a dream into practice. As the report from *The Times* noted, the event was marked not so much with sadness as with a militant sense of resolve (a resolve that found expression in heroic, political tunes): 'A number of purple banners were carried, bearing inscriptions such as "Fight on and God will give the victory", "Thoughts have gone forth whose power can sleep no more", and "Dulce et decorum est pro patria mori", and a band accompanied each section playing either a Dead March or the Marseillaise.'[12]

We all know of Wilfred Owen's sardonic appropriation of the lines from Horace that glorify dying in battle in the cause of one country, but here was an equally radical subversion. The Latin words had been inscribed in the same year of 1913 on the wall of the chapel at the Royal Military Academy at Sandhurst. At Davison's funeral patriarchal empire-building bombast became redeployed to rail against gender inequality, in as subversive a move as the ingenious re-use to which suffragettes put London's conservative street furniture.

View of the neoclassical St Pancras Church (historically referred to as St Pancras New Church), on the corner of Euston Road and Upper Woburn Place.

Chapter 5   **Timing**

> The clock of New Saint Pancras Church struck twelve, and the
> Foundling, with laudable politeness, did the same ten minutes after-
> wards, Saint something else struck the quarter.[1]

In his short story 'The Boarding House' (1834), Dickens registers a
kind of contention or disagreement over time between the various
church clocks in the Bloomsbury local soundscape. Those different
chimes, politely but firmly contradicting each other about the
precise hour, were doubtless a feature of the neighbourhood that
had been noticed by the writer at first hand as he walked through
it as a youth on his way to work at Warren's Blacking Factory in
the Strand from his lodgings in Camden. We may intuit Dickens
would have had some sense of which of these clocks was the more
correct. Commuters tend to have a fairly strong sense of timing.

The polite contention was still in play nearly a century later. The
novelist Dorothy Richardson noticed the same phenomenon when
she lived in Bloomsbury throughout the 1890s and 1900s – actually
opposite the poet W. B. Yeats in Woburn Walk in 1905 and 1906.
At one point in her novel *Interim* (1919), her autobiographical
avatar character Miriam notes Bloomsbury's temporal uncertainty
around the moment of the midnight of a New Year, a moment that
precipitates a special sonic street-life festival that she realises must
be some kind of local custom:

> Just in front of her, a single neat warning tap sounded in the air,
> touching the quick of her mind . . . St Pancras clock – striking down

the chimney . . . She ran across to the dark lattice and flung it open. In the air hung the echo of the first deep boom from Westminster. St Pancras and the nearer clocks were telling themselves off against it. They would have finished long before Big Ben came to an end. Which was midnight? Let it be St Pancras. She counted swiftly backwards; four strokes . . . Out in the darkness the dark world was turning away from darkness. Within the spaces of the night the surface of a daylit landscape gleamed for an instant titled lengthways across the sky . . . Little sounds came snapping faintly up through the darkness from the street below, voices and the creaking open of doors. Windows being pushed open up and down the street. The new year changed to a soft moonlit breath stealing through the darkness, brimming over the faces at the doors and windows, touching their brows with fingers of dawn, sending fresh soothing healing fingers in amongst their hair . . . Eleven . . . twelve . . . Across the rushing scale of St Pancras bells came a fearful clangour. Bicycle bells, cab whistles, dinner bells, the banging of tea-trays and gongs . . . Of course . . . New Year . . . it must be a Bloomsbury custom. She had had her share in a Bloomsbury New Year. Rather jolly . . . rowdy; but jolly in that sort of way . . .[2]

Interim is a novel whose title gives away one of its chief themes – that of human temporality. Serialised in the small-circulation modernist magazine *Little Review*, in which *Ulysses* was simultaneously appearing, Richardson's novel is like Joyce's more famous experimental text in that it also evolves new forms of writing in order to estrange the reader from their normative subjective experience of time. One of the inventors of what is sometimes called 'stream of consciousness' narration, Richardson's residency in Bloomsbury amidst the locality's undecided temporality may have surreptitiously nudged her towards her topic.

Punctuated by the chimes of Big Ben, *Mrs Dalloway* is another novel by a Bloomsbury-based writer which is partly set in the locality, in which time moves from the background of the narrative to become one of its major themes. Like Richardson's work, the intersection of a particular embodied consciousness with a sensuous Bloomsbury street life allows Woolf to draw the reader into a consideration of time itself. Peter Walsh is walking through Bloomsbury on his way to Clarissa's party when he hears an ambulance, which prompts a turn in his train of thought back to India, and to the rub between feelings and 'civilisation'. It dawns on the careful reader that the ambulance is racing to attend – too late, of course – to the fatally wounded body of Septimus Smith, who has just thrown himself out of his Bloomsbury boarding-house window on to the railings below. Bloomsbury's ambulance station, one of only six in the city at the time, had opened in 1916 in Herbrand Street, and Woolf's insertion of the detail marks her out as a local resident, equally alert to the particular aural phenomena of Bloomsbury's dynamic present as Richardson had been in her novel published a few years earlier.

In the passage above, Richardson's narrator is referring to St Pancras New Church, of course, but the name St Pancras also carries with it the idea of the railway station just across the road, along with a sense of a very different relation to time. Railway time – that of the twenty-four-hour clock, tangible timetables and an ever-present sense of promptitude or tardiness – was, through the three enormous stations on Bloomsbury's borders, at least as important a temporal species to the area as the eccentric debate between local churches that Dickens and Richardson each record. A hyped-up version of what the historian E. P. Thompson famously called 'industrial time', Bloomsbury's early adoption of 'railway time' meant that it was at the forefront of a shift in social temporality which grew throughout the nineteenth century in Britain and pointed towards a universalised, standardised temporality that has, in the late twentieth and twenty-first centuries, become globalised.

When in Jules Verne's *Around the World in Eighty Days* (1872) Phineas Fogg returns to London in an attempt to win his famous gentlemanly bet, it is entirely appropriate that he arrives at Euston station. That he misses the key train he needs to catch and arrives at the club five minutes late dramatises impeccably the stresses

Euston station and hotel in the 1950s. Photograph by G. Davies. Built between 1834 and 1837, this was the first London terminus for a mainline railway. The station was demolished and rebuilt in the 1960s.

and strains of the new temporalities associated with what was then the most temporally modern city in the world. In Verne's clever twist, Fogg has actually mistaken the date, having gained an extra day by circumnavigating the globe and therefore crossing the International Date Line. This *coup de théâtre* neatly gestures to the way the kind of temporal hyper-precision found in Bloomsbury was destined to be exported to places on the other side of the globe.

Another novel, written just over a decade later, also made use of Euston station and Bloomsbury in order to dramatise the frenetic, inexorable pace of modern industrialised temporality. In *The Dynamiter* (1885), co-written by Robert Louis Stevenson and his wife Fanny, a female Fenian terrorist sends her gullible lover, Harry Desborough, to Euston in a cab with a parcel that has a ticking bomb in it, unbeknownst to him. In a long description of the short journey from Queen Square to Euston, the narrator milks the dramatic irony produced by the discrepancy between the reader's awareness of the preciousness of what might be Desborough's last few minutes alive and his own sense of the tediousness of a cab ride with only the 'dumb companion' of the mysterious parcel for company:

> The streets were scarcely awake; there was little to amuse the eye; and the young man's attention centred on the dumb companion of his drive. A card was nailed upon one side, bearing the superscription: 'Miss Doolan, passenger to Dublin. Glass. With care.' . . . He gave ear; and over and above the jolting of the wheels upon the road, he was conscious of a certain regular and quiet sound that seemed to issue from the box. He put his ear to the cover; at one moment, he seemed to perceive a delicate ticking: the next, the sound was gone, nor could his closest hearkening recapture it. He laughed at himself; but still the gloom continued; and it was with more than the common relief of an arrival that he leaped from the cab before the station.[3]

At Euston station, Harry Desborough is commanded to return with the parcel to his house in Queen Square, after his lover regrets her

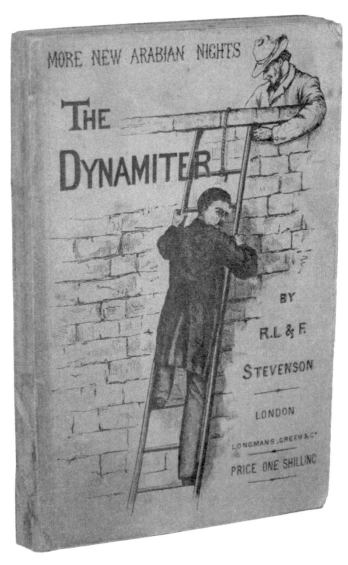

MORE NEW ARABIAN NIGHTS

THE DYNAMITER

BY
R.L & F.
STEVENSON

LONDON
LONGMANS, GREEN & C°
PRICE ONE SHILLING

Front cover of R.L. and F. Stevenson, *The Dynamiter*, Longmans, Green & Co. 1885.

plan to dynamite a moving train. There follows a tense scene in which Desborough finally realises what is going on – too late – but *The Dynamiter* is a comic novel and so the bomb fails to go off:

And then from the box that lay so quietly in the corner, a sudden catch was audible, like the catch of a clock before it strikes the hour. For one second the two stared at each other with lifted brows and stony eyes. Then Harry, throwing one arm over his face, with the other clutched the girl to his breast and staggered against the wall.

A dull and startling thud resounded through the room; their eyes blinked against the coming horror; and still clinging together like drowning people, they fell to the floor. Then followed a prolonged and strident hissing as from the indignant pit; an offensive stench seized them by the throat; the room was filled with dense and choking fumes.[4]

Both Verne's novel about the new ease of global travel and the Stevensons's about the new global threat of terrorism are also, more covertly, novels about deadlines. The deadline is a temporal horizon that constantly haunts the waking lives of novelists, as it does the other kinds of people who are most prominently associated with Bloomsbury. Academics, students and writers of all varieties enjoy an unusual degree of autonomy about how they choose to 'use their time', but it is usually paid for with the cost of a variably successful internalised ticking clock, counting down the months, weeks, minutes and seconds before time is up and whatever they have been writing has to be submitted to whoever is going to publish or mark it.

The particular feature of 'industrial time', so prevalent in Bloomsbury, that is the deadline also produces a kind of equal and opposite by-product – what we might call 'bohemian time'. The kinds of people in which Bloomsbury has traditionally specialised often adopt a very public posture of insouciance towards the ticking clock, allowing themselves a kind of temporal flexibility that is much less frequently available to workers in other parts of the city. A quick drink after a day researching or writing in one of Bloomsbury's libraries often has a curious tendency to morph into an all-nighter, the unusual room for manoeuvre within the working schedules of the novelist, the PhD student or the lecturer on sabbatical leading to the adoption of what to other Londoners might seem very odd hours.

Thomas Burke consciously exploits the odd hours of Bloomsbury in his gothic crime novella *The Bloomsbury Wonder* (1929). The main character, Stephen Trink, is an intellectual who predictably 'attends all [the] clique and coterie gatherings – teas, dinners, Bloomsbury salons, private views'. Trink seems on the surface to be entirely the 'common type' for the locality in which he lives, until he turns out to be a Satanic mass-murderer. One of the 'queer' aspects of his personality that Bloomsbury's general 'oddity' gives cover for is what the novel calls his 'Japanese ideas of time': 'A promise to call one evening about seven meant an appearance at any time between six and midnight. A "look-in" often meant that he would stay for four or five hours, and an arrangement to dine and spend the evening often meant that he would look-in for ten minutes and then abruptly disappear without a word about dinner.'[5]

For Burke, Bloomsbury's lax temporality was key to its association with genius, reflecting simultaneously what he saw to be the area's licence and madness. As he says in his memoirs about being a resident in the neighbourhood, *Living in Bloomsbury*:

> If, at three o'clock in the morning, should you need nourishment, you can go out in pyjamas to one of the all-night snack bars, and you will be served. You can go about with straws in your hair, and nobody will notice any change . . . you can go out in your wife's bedgown; and it will not matter. Bloomsbury has seen madder things than you.[6]

This bohemian temporality, with its emphasis on spontaneity and 'living in the moment', was a breath of fresh air to C. L. R. James when he lived in the area as a student, coming as he did from Trinidad, a place with a much more conservative and socially policed sense of time. In his *Letters from London* he anatomises a typical Bloomsbury day, precisely in order to suggest quite how atypical its compressed, heightened and yet entirely bohemian temporality had been to him before he moved to the area:

> At ten o'clock the beer and the cigarettes were finished and it was time to do something. A typical Bloomsbury problem. What's to be done now. We would take a taxi and go to his room. I said no, I was tired, it was best for me to go to bed, but I would walk with them to the taxi rank. When we reached the girl got in and we shook hands. 'Good night', I said. 'Oh come along, oh come with us please', still holding my hand, and with the boyfriend pushing me in from in front, I went in. We reached his room at about eleven. To do what? Not a blessed thing but to sit before a fire and talk and read again . . . This is the sort of thing that is happening day after day. That is, of course, if you want it.[7]

For C. L. R. James the idea of Bloomsbury's temporal bohemianism is bound up inextricably with what one is doing – and not doing – with one's odd hours. Classically, the 'typical Bloomsbury problem' of working out what to do with the 'now' is solved by staying up late doing things that in other parts of the city would simply constitute wasting time, i.e. talking and reading. The compelling lure of good conversation with well-read, intelligent individuals is, indeed, the fuel that keeps the fire of bohemianism burning in Bloomsbury and occasionally prevents people from going to bed when, as productive citizens, they probably should. This real-time art of talking is something distinctive about the culture of Bloomsbury.

For V. S. Pritchett, the Bloomsbury of Woolf and of academia somehow managed miraculously to revive the conversational practices of the eighteenth century, an age before the industrialisation of time had brought the ticking clock distractingly into everyone's minds:

> the eighteenth century lay down a manner of talk that has never quite died. There have been pockets of it, and it was, in fact, considerably

THE ISLAND
OF
DR MOREAU

H. G. WELLS

Front cover of H. G. Wells, *The Island of Dr Moreau*, Heinemann, Stone & Kimball 1896.

revived in the twenties in Bloomsbury and the Universities. Good London talk – if we can risk a definition – is, before anything else, light, sociable, discursive, enquiring, personal without vulgar reserves, prone to fantasy, never too serious, avoids entering the wilderness of the merely informative, the expert, and the didactic – a bore is the man who tells you everything – does not lay down the law except as a matter of personal idiosyncrasy, and is regarded as a relaxation and not as a means to an end.[8]

Through the mixture of industrial and bohemian temporalities sustained by the area, Bloomsbury has evolved a fascinatingly conflicted relation to the present moment. It has also been the part of London most given to probing the past and speculating about the future. A number of influential historians have lived here, exploiting the kind of portal its many archives offer into the thoughts and feelings of dead men and women through access to written documents. Scientists associated with Bloomsbury have also contributed to the vast elongation of time backwards, moreover. In his search for the origin of the species, for instance, the work of Charles Darwin, who lived in Gower Street in the early 1840s, reduced the span of an individual human life by comparison with the millions of years the idea of evolution brought into view.

Bloomsbury has also been peculiarly associated with the active imagination of, and preparation for, 'the shape of things to come' – a phrase H. G. Wells employed for the title of one his many futuristic novels. Wells was a student of chemistry at University College London in the late 1880s, and a number of his science fictions make use of Bloomsbury, including *The Island of Doctor Moreau* (1896) and *The Invisible Man* (1897), drawing upon his sense that if the future were to be grasped anywhere it would be there. Wells was particularly interested in the kinds of changes future societies might experience as a result of inventions in technology, but the analysis of revolutionary political thinkers such as Karl Marx emphasised instead the potential for social relations to evolve radically through systemic political change.

Though Marx famously never put to pen what a post-revolutionary society might look like, his work is throughout infused with a profound insistence that the future will be entirely different from the present. Written largely in the British Museum reading room, his theories continue to inspire activists around the world with a sense that the future is a human construction being continually forged by the dynamic agent of history, an active present in which we all play a part, whether we like it or not.

Many of Bloomsbury's very different kinds of time-related intellectual activities have taken place in and around the British Museum. As E. V. Lucas says, the institution educates its visitors about human time itself, regardless of the attention they pay to any particular exhibits: 'The British Museum is the history of the world . . . The lesson of the British Museum is the transitoriness of man and the littleness of his greatest deeds. That is the burden of its every Bloomsbury room. The ghosts of dead peoples, once dominant, inhabit it; the dust of empires fills its air.'[9]

Before the museum quarter was developed in South Kensington, the British Museum contained not only artefacts from ancient civilisations but also exhibited the natural history of the world, as this piece of doggerel, published in 1871 in the periodical *Fun*, records:

> . . . there's so great a
> Display of strata,
> And fossil creatures
> Such as here are drawn,
> And busts of Neroes,
> And other heroes,–
> You can't see their features,
> 'Cause the heads are gone.[10]

In the poem, the fossils of extinct animals and the effaced statues of the heroes of fallen empires are all mixed up, as if the museum were a kind of temporal miscellany or lucky dip in deep time. Behind the humour presented by the apparent random collection

View of the Hellenic Room at the British Museum, including the Elgin Marbles. Nineteenth-century photograph by C. Bernieri Caldesi & Co.

of these items from the past, however, contemporary controversies lurk. Extinct animals were in the 1870s still a dynamic destabilising force, acting to challenge literalist interpretations of the Bible, a book that conspicuously failed to include any mention of dinosaurs. The reference to the feature-less faces of statues, moreover, points us to what have always been the most controversial of the many objects to be found in the British Museum, now or then – the Parthenon (or Elgin) marbles, which originally adorned buildings on the Acropolis in Athens. Since 1801, when Thomas Bruce, 7th Earl of Elgin, obtained them, these classical Greek sculptures, dating from *c*. 447 to 438 BC, have been an intermittent source of tension.

From 1816 the marbles have been exhibited in Bloomsbury, after Parliament decided to purchase them from the nation. Their presence in Britain has always been the object of critique, most famously from the poet Lord Byron, who used several poems, including 'The Curse of Minerva' (1811), to protest their transferal from Greece as an inexcusable instance of cultural appropriation and a stain upon his nation's conscience. Several poets have drawn upon the marbles in less explicitly political ways, being inspired by them to think about the passing of time, as John Keats did, in his 'On Seeing the Elgin Marbles' (1817):

My spirit is too weak – mortality
　　Weighs heavily on me like unwilling sleep,
　　And each imagined pinnacle and steep
Of godlike hardship tells me I must die
Like a sick eagle looking at the sky.
　　Yet 'tis a gentle luxury to weep
　　That I have not the cloudy winds to keep
Fresh for the opening of the morning's eye.
Such dim-conceived glories of the brain
　　Bring round the heart an undescribable feud;
So do these wonders a most dizzy pain,
　　That mingles Grecian grandeur with the rude
Wasting of old time – with a billowy main –
　　A sun – a shadow of a magnitude.[11]

In this poem, the sight of the statues provokes in the poet a visceral sense of an ending – that is, his own, in death. Yet behind the overt theme of a personal encounter with 'mortality', there are also implicit nods to the wider politics in which the Elgin marbles were then, as now, embroiled. Keats wrote this sonnet having gone to see the marbles with his friend, the painter Benjamin Haydon, earlier in the day. Haydon had been one of the most passionate advocates for the nation's purchase of the sculptures, but Keats's poem reflects less his friend's enthusiasm than a deeply conflicted reaction, mixing wonder at the 'Grecian grandeur' he has witnessed with a 'dizzy' apprehension of the 'undescribable feud' the presence of these statues had recently provoked in the British public sphere. That richly ambiguous phrase – 'the rude/ Wasting of old time' – conjures the poet's sense of the multiple temporalities that cluster around these transplanted objects. The ruined remains of an ancient, pre-Christian world, after all, confront the nineteenth-century Briton not only with a sense of their own personal mortality, but with a sense of the transitory nature of all political power.

Another poet known for thematising the passage of time who was fascinated by the Elgin marbles is Thomas Hardy. His 'In the British Museum' plays with the almost clichéd idea that the sculptures transport viewers back to ancient times, but does so in order to raise troubling questions about the potential meaningless of the present moment. Apostrophising a viewer of the marbles, rather than the statues themselves, Hardy offers no solution to the problem he poses about the way time appears to erode all human achievement:

> What do you see in that time-touched stone,
> When nothing is there
> But ashen blankness, although you give it
> A rigid stare?[12]

Interestingly, throughout the nineteenth century, while many visitors to the museum would continue to give a 'rigid stare', rather

Horse head fragment from the Elgin Marbles at the British Museum. Nineteenth-century photograph by C. Bernieri Caldesi & Co.

emptily, at the 'ashen blankness' of the transplanted sculptures, other people would been treating the marbles to a much more dynamic, productive gaze. From the moment they were displayed there, the marbles played a major role in British art pedagogy. In lieu of living models, the lifeless figures were studied by young artists, like the teenager Millais, who learnt to draw by copying what was seen as the perfect physical form. Crystallising notions of athletic male beauty derived from Hellenic culture that evolved throughout the nineteenth century into the cult of sport and athleticism that dominates ideals of masculine physicality today, the marbles might be seen to exert a kind of influence that reaches far beyond either the place of their original or their latter exhibition. In a strange sense, that influence can be felt in the industrialised temporality that pervades modern gyms throughout the world, in the 'reps' of men and women who pump iron with machinic regularity, straining to perfect in their own bodies a more ideal product.

When a character in Hardy's lesser-known novel *The Hand of Ethelberta* (1876) goes to the British Museum, the historical artefacts seem to effect a kind of time travel: 'Only just think that this is not imagined of Assyria, but done in Assyrian times by Assyrian hands. Don't you feel as if you were actually in Nineveh; that we not walk between these slabs, so walked Ninevites between them once?'[13] This idea of the museum as a space of time travel is dramatised more literally, in a way that underlines the political controversy that attends its exhibits, in Edith Nesbit's *The Story of the Amulet* (1906). Best known today for *The Railway Children*, Nesbit was a committed Fabian, and many of her novels perform an implicit left-wing politics, socialist and anti-imperialist in flavour. *The Story of the Amulet*, the last book of the Psammead trilogy, features an episode in the British Museum that centres upon the ancient artefacts there but draws out a message from them that is clearly intended to speak to the present moment.

In one scene, the children use the magical amulet of the book's title to bring an ancient Babylonian queen to modern London. Reasoning that the British Museum is the one metropolitan

Illustration in E. Nesbit, *The Story of the Amulet*, T. Fisher Unwin, 1906.

institution at which their guest will be able to see things from her own country, they take her there. When she complains that the items she sees displayed have been stolen from her, and attempts to reclaim them as her rightful possessions, she is mistaken for a 'poor, demented thing' and asked to leave the premises. Taking revenge, she makes a wish that 'all those Babylonian things . . . come out to me here – slowly, so that those dogs and slaves can see the working of the great Queen's magic'. The narrative continues:

> Next moment there was a crash. The glass swing doors and all their framework were smashed suddenly and completely. The crowd of angry gentlemen sprang aside when they saw what had done this.
>
> But the nastiest of them was not quick enough, and he was roughly pushed out of the way by an enormous stone bull that was floating steadily through the door. It came and stood beside the Queen in the middle of the courtyard.
>
> It was followed by more stone images, by great slabs of carved stone, bricks, helmets, tools, weapons, fetters, wine-jars, bowls, bottles, vases, jugs, saucers, seals, and the round long things, something like rolling pins with marks on them like the print of little bird-feet, necklaces, collars, rings, armlets, earrings – heaps and heaps and heaps of things, far more than anyone had time to count, or even to see distinctly.[14]

In this spectacular event, the 'angry' keepers of the museum are pushed roughly aside by the expropriated objects as they return to their owner. The museum here stands for empire itself, carefully concealing its own repressed violent histories behind glass doors and, through its air of complacent calm, projecting a permanence when its power is inevitably only temporary.

In addition to the conservative function performed by the museum in maintaining a tidy non-threatening version of the past – for the passive consumption of privileged metropolitans in the present – in the nineteenth and for much of the twentieth century the same building also hosted political thinkers like Karl Marx, whose writings in its reading room were active in the disruption of that present and the imagination of a revolutionary future. This

'It Was Followed by More Stone Images.' Illustration by H. R. Millar, in E. Nesbit, *The Story of the Amulet*, T. Fisher Unwin, 1906.

future-orientated quality of the museum is perhaps most fully imagined in William Morris's *News from Nowhere*, in which a radical writer goes to bed in late nineteenth-century Hammersmith and wakes up in the twenty-second century. The middle third of the novel is set in and around the British Museum, and it is appropriately in the context of that temporally complex location that readers learn the revolutionary history of the utopian society.

Angela Carter's *Nights at the Circus* (1984) makes a nod to the museum's role in imagining the historical future. Towards the end of the novel, Jack Walser, the male journalist who follows the legendary winged lady, Fevvers, around the world in an attempt to write an exposé of her art, reads a letter that admits he has been his subject's dupe:

> Those letters we sent home by you in the diplomatic bag were news of the struggle in Russia to comrades in exile, written in invisible ink, so we made most grievous use of you, I'm sorry to say, for if the secret police had found out about it, you'd have been sent to Siberia somewhere we couldn't find you. But Liz *would* do it, having made a promise to a spry little gent with a 'tache she met in the reading-room of the British Museum.
>
> Furthermore, we played a trick on you with the aid of Nelson's clock the first night we met . . . but the clock is gone and I'll play tricks on you no more.[15]

Unbeknownst to him, Walser has been carrying subversive missives in and out of Tsarist Russia, at the behest of an exiled political figure who plots revolutions from the reading room of the British Museum, like Marx and then Lenin did. In linking this 'trick' with the other tricks Fevvers has played upon Walser's sense of time, Carter pays subtle homage to the complex, interwoven temporalities of Bloomsbury's central institution when it was at the height of its powers.

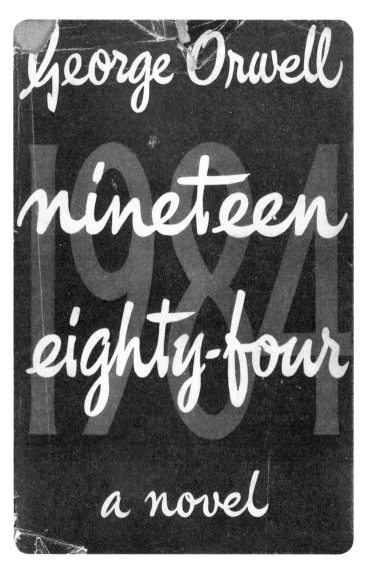

Front cover of George Orwell, *Nineteen Eighty-Four*. 1st edition. Secker & Warburg, 1949.

Chapter 6 **Wording**

For the duration of the Second World War the British government's department for propaganda, the Ministry of Information, was located in Senate House, the central building of the University of London and the location of its humanities libraries. The sheer inhuman scale of Holden's enormous art-deco tower seems to have chimed with the kinds of authoritarian activities that went on inside it in wartime. In his Blitz spy novel, *The Ministry of Fear* (1943), Graham Greene rechristens the department in order to underline its sinister, totalitarian overtones. When George Orwell, whose wife Eileen worked in the ministry's Censorship division in the early 1940s, included a version of this special branch of the civil service in his terrifying political fantasy *Nineteen Eighty-Four* (1949), he renamed it as the Ministry of Truth, or Minitrue. In *Nineteen Eighty-Four*, a huge pyramid-like building of white concrete towers over the city, containing thousands of offices dedicated to falsifying historical records and to disseminating an invented language called Newspeak, a language composed of words that have been specially designed to facilitate 'doublethink' in the population.

Both Greene's and Orwell's fictional responses to the Ministry of Information conspicuously tweaked its name. In so doing they hinted at the ways in which the Bloomsbury office they depicted was itself in the business of monitoring and manipulating words. By invoking memories of the real Ministry of Information in his fictional dystopia, Orwell doubtless intended to raise the irony that a space dedicated in

Exterior view of Senate House, April 2017.

ordinary times to academic freedom could be repurposed so easily by an unaccountable state for something like its polar opposite.

From another perspective, however, the use of the enormous tower of Senate House in the Second World War as a site for overseeing of the use of English was entirely appropriately placed in the heart of Bloomsbury. Through its centrality to several professions that have a self-conscious and dynamic purchase upon language and its meaning – law, publishing, academia and literature – Bloomsbury had been in the business of monitoring and manipulating words long before its first skyscraper was commandeered in the 1940s. To have located their wartime department responsible for language usage in Senate House, the British government might be seen to have been responding to what was, and continues to be, the local skill set.

That said, Bloomsbury's professional relation to the English language has rarely carried such authoritarian resonances as it did when Orwell's wife worked for the Ministry of Information. Indeed, Bloomsbury's specialist attention to, and scrutiny of, words has worked to open up and free language as often as it has tried to restrict it. Two kinds of language survey to have been conducted in Bloomsbury exemplify this alternative approach particularly well. Both are ongoing projects, which respond to the endlessly open-ended evolution of language itself.

The Survey of English Usage, still based in the department of English Language and Literature in UCL, was the first research centre in Europe to make use of 'corpora' – large bodies of ordinary conversations transcribed, annotated and filed – in their analysis of language use as it was actually spoken. Now computerised, when the survey was founded in 1959 by Randolph Quirk, all the work was done by a laborious multi-stage process of recording on reel-to-reel tapes, which were typed up, then filed and indexed physically. Corpus linguistics is grounded in a radically non-judgemental relationship to language that emerged from the discipline's inception, at a point in history when British universities were in general reorienting

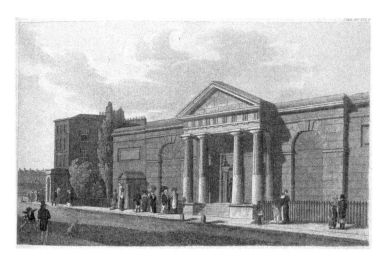

'Russell Institution, Great Coram Street.' Plate 35 from *R. Ackerman's Repository of Arts*, 1811.

themselves away from the conservation of elite knowledge towards an engagement with the masses for progressive ends.

More than a century before, however, Bloomsbury had also been the site for the production of another important English language survey project, though one that was pursued by one man alone – the construction of the first modern thesaurus. Peter Mark Roget (1779–1869) was living in 18 Upper Bedford Place, when he published his *Thesaurus of English Words and Phrases* (1852). As a physician, Roget had been an influential force within medicine from the time he moved to London in the early 1800s. In Bloomsbury he contributed popular lectures on animal physiology to the Russell Literary and Scientific Institution as early as 1809, helped found and contributed treatises for the Society for the Diffusion of Useful Knowledge, and served on the senate of the university from the late 1830s until his death.

Despite these other achievements, however, the thesaurus that bears Roget's name deserves to be regarded as his most significant feat. Roget begun the process of accumulating, grouping and linking words in his youth, but it was only after giving up his extensive medical and scientific duties that he could find time to organise and build upon what he had done. Here, in its preface, Roget is very clear about how much labour went into his retirement project:

> I had often, during that long interval, found this little collection, scanty and imperfect as it was, of much use to me in literary composition, and often contemplated its extension and improvement; but a sense of the magnitude of the task, amidst a multitude of other avocations, deterred me from the attempt. Since my retirement from the duties of Secretary of the Royal Society, however, finding myself possessed of more leisure, and believing that a repertory of which I had myself experienced the advantage might, when amplified, prove useful to others, I resolved to embark on an undertaking, which, for the last three or four years, has given me incessant occupation, and has, indeed, imposed upon me an amount of labour very much greater than I had anticipated.[1]

Even as Roget stresses quite how much work went into its compilation, the Preface also clearly underlines that the thesaurus is not primarily about him. His list of words, much amplified and extended, is, after all, a 'collection' rather than a 'literary composition'; a survey that draws upon the social resource of English language, which will be 'useful to others' even as it has been of 'much use' in his own writing. Impelled by the same democratic spirit of the mid-nineteenth century that diffused knowledge and combatted illiteracy through increasing access to education, the thesaurus split reviewers on political lines. While the radical *Westminster Review* said in 1853, 'Roget will rank with Samuel Johnson as a literary instrument-maker of the first-class', the more conservative *Athenaeum* warned that good writers should be in no need of such a 'crutch'.[2]

According to his biographer Joshua Kendall, Roget the doctor and scientist thought that 'specious phraseology' spread 'prejudice and error'.[3] He compiled the thesaurus in order to combat the imprecise use of language, rather than simply to expand its users' vocabularies. This imperative links Roget with the argument Orwell made in his essay 'Politics and the English Language' (1946), which dates from the same period as *Nineteen Eighty-Four*, and shares its anxieties about what damage improperly chosen words can do. Underlining the responsibility that we all have to deploy words carefully, Orwell suggests that 'specious phraseology' has a key role in justifying the unconscionable:

> In our time, political speech and writing are largely the defence of the indefensible. Things like the continuance of British rule in India, the Russian purges and deportations, the dropping of the atom bombs on Japan, can indeed be defended, but only by arguments which are too brutal for most people to face, and which do not square with the professed aims of political parties. Defenceless villages are bombarded from the air, the inhabitants driven out into the countryside, the cattle machine-gunned, the huts set on fire with incendiary bullets: this is called *pacification*. Millions of peasants are robbed

Photographic portrait of Peter Mark Roget, in T. H. Barker [ed.], *Photographs of Eminent Medical Men of all Countries, with Brief Analytical Notices of Their Works … The photographic portraits from life by Ernest Edwards etc.* J. Churchill & Sons 1867..

of their farms and sent trudging along the roads with no more than they can carry: this is called *transfer of population* or *rectification of frontiers*. People are imprisoned for years without trial, or shot in the back of the neck or sent to die of scurvy in Arctic lumber camps: this is called *elimination of unreliable elements*. Such phraseology is needed if one wants to name things without calling up mental pictures of them.[4]

Bloomsbury has always been dominated by different word-wielding professions that have known the material efficacy of phraseology. All of these professions have made ample use of 'literary instruments' like the thesaurus – and, more broadly, education. Turning these 'crutches' into something more like weapons, writers of all kinds writing in Bloomsbury have harnessed the power of language for very different causes, achieving influence through their command of their own words, and the words of others, for good or ill. The neighbourhood's impact on the world has indeed been primarily through language.

One of the wordy activities that has consistently been associated with Bloomsbury is publishing. Today, some very fine townhouses in Bedford Square play host, appropriately, to the publishing house known as Bloomsbury, a prestigious address the company could afford only after the windfall they received with the runaway success of their author J. K. Rowling's bestselling Harry Potter series. In a crude sense, the appearance of Rowling herself in the *Sunday Times* Rich List is one very clear testament to the material power of words to effect change. In a BBC interview from 2001, Rowling admits she was thinking of Euston when she chose King's Cross railway station for her magical supplementary platform 9¾, from which the young wizard departs north for Hogwarts. In the film adaptations, to add more confusion to the question of its whereabouts, the crew preferred the grand architecture of neighbouring St Pancras, shooting there instead of the humbler setting specified in the book. In a way it seems appropriate that all three of the railway stations bordering the Euston Road find their way into the Harry Potter

Poet, dramatist, literary critic and publisher T. S. Eliot. Photograph by John Gay, 1950.

myth, however. Bloomsbury has been such an important space for Rowling, through her productive relationship with the publishing company that bears the neighbourhood's name.

Rowling's debt to Bloomsbury publishing, and their debt to her, presents an image of reciprocal appreciation between writers and publishers that is, of course, only half the picture. The publishing industry is, after all, much more frequently involved in rejecting manuscripts than in championing them. Famously, for example, Orwell's masterpiece *Animal Farm* was rejected by probably the most influential person to work in publishing in the locality to date – T. S. Eliot, who worked at Faber & Faber (based in Russell Square and then Queen Square, and now found in Great Russell Street).

Faber's heyday began when Eliot, known widely at the time as the 'Pope of Russell Square', joined its staff in the 1920s having left Lloyds Bank. A kind of St Peter-like gatekeeper upon British literary culture, he exerted considerable influence upon the canon, not only through his publishing and editorial decisions, but also through his literary criticism, which appeared in the Faber-published modernist periodical *Criterion*.

At the heart of the Faber list, as it developed under Eliot's careful watch, was poetry. As the years progressed, the illustrious roll call came to include not only high modernists, such as Ezra Pound, James Joyce and Wyndham Lewis, but also representatives of the more overtly left-wing grouping to have emerged in the 1930s, such as W. H. Auden, Stephen Spender and Louis MacNeice.

Eliot's gatekeeping work – in rejecting some manuscripts and heavily editing others – was often done with one eye to censorship. As a letter to the owner Geoffrey Faber, from April 1936, urging the publication of Djuna Barnes's sexually dissident and formally experimental masterpiece *Nightwood* suggests, Eliot was aware of his responsibility to help his authors' important work negotiate the exclusionary powers of the censors: 'I am perpetually being shocked by what doesn't shock other people, and not being shocked by what does shock other people.' Taking care to ensure that this novel about lesbianism and cross-dressing would not be censored

C 1878   76

THE LADIES' PRINTING PRESS,
(For the Tuition and Employment of Necessitous Gentlewomen,)

48 HUNTER STREET, BRUNSWICK SQUARE, W.C.

Printers in Ordinary to

The Royal Family.

NEW MUSIC.

Subscribers may have any of the following select pieces of Music at 1s. each.

ALL HAIL, THOU NEW YEAR—Song.
WELCOME MERRY CHRISTMAS—Part Song.
A NEW YEAR'S LAY—Song.
GOD BLESS THE CHURCH—Song.
{ DEAD MARCH.
{ MARCH IN "OCCASIONAL ORATORIO."
{ MINUET IN "SAMSON."
{ PASTORAL SYMPHONY—"MESSIAH."
{ A FESTIVAL MARCH.
{ DYING CHILD AND HIS MOTHER.—Song.
AUTUMN—Song.
BRIDAL MARCH.
BRIGHT, BEAUTIFUL SPRING—Song.
CHARITY—Song.
{ HARVEST MARCH.
{ HARVEST HOME OF EARTH—Solo and Chorus.
HARVEST—Part Song.
LOVE ME LITTLE, LOVE ME LONG—Song.
MAY DAY—Part Song.
OH, THE SWEET CONTENTMENT—Song.
OLD COTTAGE CLOCK—Song.
ROGER'S COURTSHIP—Duet and Chorus.
TEARS THAT EXHALE—Solo and Chorus.
THERE'S NOTHING TRUE BUT HEAVEN—Song.
WITHERING—Vocal Duet.
WEEP NOT—Song.
GOOD HUMOUR—Duet.
THE SUN AND THE BROOK—Duet.
YE PRETTY BIRDS—Song.
REMEMBER—Song.
YE DAISIES GAY—Song.
THE SERAPIS QUADRILLES.
FORGET ME NOT—Song.
TELL ME WHERE IS BEAUTY FOUND—Duet.
THE MINERVA QUADRILLES.

NEW BOOKS.

MAB: A Stirring Tale of Modern Times. Demy 8vo., cloth, gilt lettered sides and edges. Price 2s. 6d.

OVER THE WATER; A Holiday Tour. By the Author of "A Glance at Belgium and the Rhine." Demy 8vo., handsomely bound in cloth, gilt lettered side and edges. Price 5s.

CHILDREN'S TEXT-BOOK, Fcap. 4to., cloth, bevelled, gilt back, sides and edges, with Photograph, interleaved for Meditation, 7s. 6d.

EXTRACTS AND VERSES; for Strengthening and Comforting Believers. Fcap. 8vo., cloth, gilt lettered. Price 2s.

IN TIME OF TROUBLE: Being Short Extracts, Collected from the Works of the Best Authors, for the Poor in Spirit. Crown 8vo., 60 pp., in wrapper. Price 3d.

TEST OF LOVE. Crown 8vo., Price 1d. each.

HOME WORDS; an Illustrated Monthly Magazine, Price 2d.

LINES AND VERSES. By the Author of "Wild Flowers' Tea Party," and other Poems. Royal 16mo., cloth, gilt lettered side and edges. Price 2s. 6d.

THOUGHTS OF PEACE FOR GIRLS. By the Author of "The Colonist." Price 3d. ⅌ dozen, or 10s. ⅌ 100,

THE COLONIST; An Episode in Acadian History. By the Author of "Thoughts of Peace for Girls." Crown 8vo. 33 pp. Price 6d.

IDA'S DREAM. By the Author of "Scenes of Every Day Life." Crown 8vo. 200 pp. Price 1s. 6d.

BLACK AND BROWN. By the Author of "Ida's Dream," "Scenes of Every Day Life," &c. Crown 8vo., nearly 350 pp. Price, 3s.

SCENES OF EVERY DAY LIFE. By the Author of "Ida's Dream." Price 6d. ⅌ dozen.

SCRIPTURAL STUDIES OF THE SONGS OF SOLOMAN. Fcap. 8vo. Price 2s. 6d.

A FEW PLAIN WORDS ON THE TRUE, PROTESTANT, CHRISTIAN, RULE OF FAITH. Crown 8vo. Price 6d.

ETC.,   ETC.,   ETC.

.*. *Subscribers are entitled to purchase any of the above Works at a reduction of one-third below the publishing price.*

Specimens of our Music Types.

Gem. Praise ye Je ho vah!

Pearl. Praise and bless his name, for

Ruby e ver and e ver.

Late nineteenth-century advertisement for The Ladies' Printing Press, based at 48 Hunter Street, Brunswick Square. The press was part of the London Society for the Employment of Necessitous Gentlewomen.

Women compositors at The Victoria Press, Great Coram-Street. Plate from the *Illustrated London News*, 1861.

by an over-vigilant state, Eliot recognised in his editorial procedure a means by which the powerful and significant words of others could be delivered safely into the public realm: 'my feeling is that this book is very likely the last big thing to be done in our time.'[5]

Other publishing houses based in Bloomsbury have much more overt political agendas. Persephone Books, whose bookshop can today be found in Lamb's Conduit Street, for instance, taps into Bloomsbury's long relationship with feminism. A small but extremely innovative house, it specialises in unearthing undeservedly forgotten novels by twentieth-century women – it clearly sees publishing as one of the means by which voices that have been marginalised can be revalued once more. In many ways, Persephone should be seen as continuous with a much earlier feminist publishing venture to be located in Bloomsbury, the Victoria Press, which Emily Faithfull founded at 9 Coram Street in 1860. Staffing the company entirely with women, Faithfull also used the press to produce periodicals that fought explicitly for women's rights.

A number of important political publishers lived in Bloomsbury, including several European and Russian exiles who used the area as a base from which to write and release material that would have led to their imprisonment in their home countries. The examples of Marx and Lenin are well known, but another important, less famous, example is Alexander Herzen, who started up the Free Russian Press, the first independent Russian political publishers, from 38 Regent Square in 1853. Later moving to 82 Judd Street, where a plaque remembers his residency, Herzen made use of the relative freedom that Bloomsbury offered him to publish a series of polemical essays, attacking the whole system of government in Russia, and especially arguing for forms of agrarian collectivism to replace the egregious serfdom that then prevailed. His periodicals, the *Polyarnaya Zvyezda* (*Polar Star*) and the *Kolokol* (*Bell*), were highly influential within Russia, despite being illegal, and rumours circulated that the Tsar himself was a reader.

While Bloomsbury was, in the nineteenth century, used by exiles such as Herzen as a space from which to publish material whose political object was located thousands of miles away, the area was also the platform for radical publications that had much more local and more restricted aims. One important example is the *Lancet*, the pioneering medical weekly which the surgeon Thomas Wakley launched in 1823. Living for much of his life at 35 Bedford Square, Wakley used the periodical to campaign for the improvement and professionalisation of medicine, a goal he saw as inextricably linked with his other radical political concerns, which included parliamentary reform, the abolition of slavery and, significantly, the repeal of the Newspaper Stamp Act, a tax he saw as an impediment to the freedom of the press. Elected as a Radical MP for Finsbury in 1835 – the constituency to which Bloomsbury then belonged – Wakley campaigned the following year for the repeal of the stamp duty by publishing six issues of *A Voice from the Commons*, an unstamped newspaper. In terms of the *Lancet*, Wakley's persistent efforts to reform British medicine bore fruit in the Medical Act of 1858, an important piece of legislation that built the way for later improvements in the provision of healthcare throughout the country.

One of the key means by which Bloomsbury has wielded material power through its command of language is through the role of its lawyers in relation to legislation. Through their advice and advocacy, rulings and judgments, solicitors, barristers and judges deploy words in relation to specific cases that have far-reaching social consequences. As John Cordy Jeaffreson explains in his *A Book about Lawyers* (1866), Bloomsbury was in the eighteenth and early nineteenth centuries the chosen residential site for the most prestigious barristers:

> Crossing Holborn, the lawyers settled on a virgin plain beyond the ugly houses which had sprung up on the north of Great Queen Street, and on the country side of Holborn. Speedily a new quarter arose, extending from Gray's Inn on the east to Southampton Row

on the west, and lying between Holborn and the line of Ormond Street, Red Lion Street, Bedford Row, Great Ormond Street, Little Ormond Street, Great James Street, and Little James Street were amongst its best thoroughfares; in its centre was Red Lion Square, and in its northwestern corner lay Queen's Square. Steadily enlarging its boundaries, it comprised at later dates Guilford Street, John's Street, Doughty Street, Mecklenburgh Square, Brunswick Square, Bloomsbury Square, Russell Square, Bedford Square – indeed, all the region lying between Gray's Inn Lane (on the east), Tottenham Court Road (on the west), Holborn (on the south), and a line running along the north of the Foundling Hospital and 'the squares'. Of course this large residential district was more than the lawyers required for themselves. It became and long remained a favourite quarter with merchants, physicians, and surgeons; and until a recent date it comprised the mansions of many leading members of the aristocracy. But from its first commencement it was so intimately associated with the legal profession that it was often called the 'law quarter'.[6]

One of the most famous of these lawyers was a family friend of Roget's, Sir Samuel Romilly, who became Solicitor General in 1806. A liberal, he overwhelmingly reduced the number of criminal offences to carry a mandatory death sentence, and lent his support to a number of other radical causes, such as the anti-slavery movement. He was a resident of 21 Russell Square when he cut his throat, in suicidal grief at his wife's recent unexpected death. Roget was devastated, though according to a periodical from the time, his feelings were by no means uncommon, as Romilly's tireless attempts to reform Britain's brutal penal code had not gone unnoticed by the general public:

Since the day when the public was made acquainted with the fall of the immortal Nelson, we do not recollect one in which the mourning was so deep and universal as on the death of Sir Samuel Romilly; and never was there an occasion when there was a more general expression of profound sorrow in all ranks of the people.[7]

Engraving of William Murray, 1st Earl of Mansfield, in Edmund Lodge, *Portraits of Illustrious Personages of Great Britain*, 1832.

For lawyers to achieve this sort of popularity amidst 'all ranks of the people' is rare indeed. In Bloomsbury's history, the opposite has more often been the case, and the forceful words of lawyers have been met with physical violence on the neighbourhood's streets more than once. Lord Eldon's contribution to the passing of the Corn Laws in 1815 led to the riots outside his house at No. 6 Bedford Square, as the previous chapter relates. A similar scene had greeted the Bloomsbury Square house of William Murray, Earl of Mansfield (1705–93), during the Gordon Riots of 1780 – probably the most violent scene in the neighbourhood's history.

Mansfield is one of the most enduringly famous of Bloomsbury's lawyers, having been made Solicitor General at the early age of thirty-seven. His most widely known court judgment was that which made slavery effectively illegal in England, in 1772, one of a stuttering series of legislative changes that finally resulted in its more complete ban, more than half a century later. Far from being a liberal, however, it appears that Murray was not at all inclined to rule against what he saw to be the natural rights of slave-owners over their own 'property'. Finding no justification within law for slavery's continued existence, but unwilling to set any kind of precedent that might threaten the status quo, Mansfield reluctantly made his judgment only after having unsuccessfully attempted to persuade the slaver-claimant to drop a case he would inevitably lose.

In general, Mansfield's important role in English legal history depended on his innovative negotiations with the law to facilitate the expansion of global capitalism under the aegis of the British Empire. He advised colonial governors about how to avoid legal challenge, for instance, and produced what one historian has called 'legal fictions' to justify the practice of English jurisdiction in places far away from England.[8] Over the course of his career, his gift for spinning legal language to the benefit of the rich and powerful made him as wealthy as many of the merchants and businessmen who relied on him.

The Riot in Broad Street, on the Seventh of June 1780. Engraving published by John &
Joseph Boydell, London. Broad Street was roughly located in the position of the present-
day New Oxford Street.

At home, he was a highly unpopular figure, largely because of his bloodthirstiness. When he was Lord Chief Justice of the King's Bench the spikes on the King's Bench Prison walls were known as Lord Mansfield's teeth, such terror did he inspire in the general populace. At the Sessions he attended at the Old Bailey, he oversaw as many as 102 hangings, not to mention the transportation of 448 people to America. As the historian Peter Linebaugh has argued, when Mansfield's house in Bloomsbury Square was broken into during the Gordon Riots of 1780, the collective act of violence was by no means accidental or mindless. Rather, it was one of a network of attacked sites targeted precisely because of their association with a legislative and judicial system that was widely reviled. In moving on from burning down Newgate Prison to very prominently destroying Mansfield's law library, the rioters drew attention, unwittingly or otherwise, to the co-dependence of monopolised state violence and the language of power.

The attack on Mansfield's house was one of the most physically charged moments in Bloomsbury's history. Beginning with the uprooting of the railings that surrounded Bloomsbury Square, it ended, a few days later, with the gruesome spectacle of public hangings in the same space. Dickens devotes several pages to the event in *Barnaby Rudge*, his historical novel about the riots, published sixty years after they took place:

> the mob gathering round Lord Mansfield's house, had called on those within to open the door, and receiving no reply (for Lord and Lady Mansfield were at that moment escaping by the backway), forced an entrance according to their usual custom. That they then began to demolish the house with great fury, and setting fire to it in several parts, involved in a common ruin the whole of the costly furniture, the plate and jewels, a beautiful gallery of pictures, the rarest collection of manuscripts ever possessed by any one private person in the world, and worse than all, because nothing could replace this loss, the great Law Library, on almost every page of which were notes in the Judge's own hand, of inestimable value – being the results

of the study and experience of his whole life. That while they were howling and exulting round the fire, a troop of soldiers, with a magistrate among them, came up, and being too late (for the mischief was by that time done), began to disperse the crowd. That the Riot Act being read, and the crowd still resisting, the soldiers received orders to fire, and levelling their muskets shot dead at the first discharge six men and a woman, and wounded many persons; and loading again directly, fired another volley, but over the people's heads it was supposed, as none were seen to fall. That thereupon, and daunted by the shrieks and tumult, the crowd began to disperse, and the soldiers went away, leaving the killed and wounded on the ground: which they had no sooner done than the rioters came back again, and taking up the dead bodies, and the wounded people, formed into a rude procession, having the bodies in the front. That in this order they paraded off with a horrible merriment; fixing weapons in the dead men's hands to make them look as if alive; and preceded by a fellow ringing Lord Mansfield's dinner-bell with all his might.[9]

Towards the end of this passage, Dickens dwells on the most grotesque details of accounts of the riots he had read in his research for his historical novel. He fixes our attention on the way still-warm corpses are recruited to participate in parodic spectacles of the kinds of official power the law might be seen to represent. Some sort of equation is being drawn between the callous disregard paid by rioters to the recently dead bodies of their fellows, and that casual destruction of those 'notes in the Judge's own hand, of inestimable value'. But such an equation raises anxieties for the reader. Can the burning of any papers, however 'precious', really justify the massacre of human beings that follows? Reading between the lines, Dickens's evident opposition to mob mentality is accompanied by an ambivalence about the deployment of such brutal state violence to rebut the destruction of a collection of manuscripts, however rare.

Later in his career, Dickens's ambivalence about the law's complicity with the establishment in the oppression of the poor and

Halbot Knight Browne (otherwise known as Phiz), illustration of the Gordon Riots, in Charles Dickens, *Barnaby Rudge*, the Biographical Edition, 1902, with plates after the original illustrations.

the uneducated hardened into a profound distaste for Bloomsbury's most prominent non-literary wordy profession. He was living in Tavistock House, Tavistock Square, when he wrote *Bleak House* (1852–53), a novel that makes a systematic attack on barristers, the Court of Chancery and the 'foggy' language of legalese. When the illiterate crossing sweeper Jo dies, after being hounded by the forces of the law throughout the narrative, Dickens's narrator all of a sudden adopts the commanding tone of a barrister or a judge, and addresses the whole society, as if making an appeal to a jury on behalf of a wronged client: 'Dead, your Majesty. Dead, my lords and gentlemen. Dead, right reverends and wrong reverends of every order. Dead, men and women, born with heavenly compassion in your hearts. And dying thus around us every day.'[10] In a novel that consistently shows the law as corrupt and amoral, the stylistic manoeuvre is a particularly subversive one, and the effect is hard-hitting to readers even today.

One writer associated with Bloomsbury to have suffered directly from the words of lawyers also resident in the area was the poet Percy Shelley, who lodged in several streets in Bloomsbury, including what is now Marchmont Street, in 1816–17. It was when living at this address that Shelley was denied custody of his children, after the death of his wife, following the judgment of the ultra-conservative lawyer and Bloomsbury resident, Lord Eldon. Baron Denman, meanwhile, who lived for many years in No. 50 Bedford Square, was the lawyer that as Lord Chief Justice was responsible for the prosecution of the publisher of Shelley's complete works for blasphemy. The most obvious homage to Bloomsbury in Shelley's work can be found in 'Ozymandias' (1818), which muses upon the statue of Rameses II that he observed at the British Museum. But in his most famous work of prose, 'A Defence of Poetry' (1821), it is also possible to trace more obliquely the intellectual impact Shelley's Bloomsbury residency might have made upon his thinking. A radical treatise that argues for the potent value of literary language in figuring forth a new and better world, the

Photographic portrait of Charles Dickens. Watkins Studio, 1861.

'defence' very pointedly makes a 'case' for literature as a rival authority to the language of power embodied in legalese.

> For the literature of England, an energetic development of which has ever preceded or accompanied a great and free development of the national will, has arisen as it were from a new birth. In spite of the low-thoughted envy which would undervalue contemporary merit, our own will be a memorable age in intellectual achievements, and we live among such philosophers and poets as surpass beyond comparison any who have appeared since the last national struggle for civil and religious liberty. The most unfailing herald, companion, and follower of the awakening of a great people to work a beneficial change in opinion or institution, is poetry. At such periods there is an accumulation of the power of communicating and receiving intense and impassioned conceptions respecting man and nature. The persons in whom this power resides may often, as far as regards many portions of their nature, have little apparent correspondence with that spirit of good of which they are the ministers. But even whilst they deny and abjure, they are yet compelled to serve, the power which is seated on the throne of their own soul. It is impossible to read the compositions of the most celebrated writers of the present day without being startled with the electric life which burns within their words. They measure the circumference and sound the depths of human nature with a comprehensive and all-penetrating spirit, and they are themselves perhaps the most sincerely astonished at its manifestations; for it is less their spirit than the spirit of the age. Poets are the hierophants of an unapprehended inspiration; the mirrors of the gigantic shadows which futurity casts upon the present; the words which express what they understand not; the trumpets which sing to battle, and feel not what they inspire; the influence which is moved not, but moves. Poets are the unacknowledged legislators of the world.[11]

For Shelley, the language of poets and writers had a power just as real as that of politicians and lawyers, in that it could create new worlds beyond the limitations of the present one. Perhaps his understanding of the rival jurisdictions of law and literature emerged from his experience of a part of London in which the two word-wielding professions cohabited in the same streets and squares.

John Cordy Jeaffreson relates that, in the early nineteenth century, Bloomsbury was so heavily associated with lawyers that it was known by some as the 'law quarter' of London. Nowadays it is much more likely to be known as a 'literary quarter' – although few writers can afford to live there currently, of course. A list of famous novelists to have lived in Bloomsbury at some point in their lives is too substantial to more than adumbrate here: Fanny Burney, Edgar Allan Poe, Charles Dickens, William Thackeray, Benjamin Disraeli, Mary Elizabeth Braddon, George Gissing, William Morris, H. G. Wells, Dorothy Richardson, Virginia Woolf and Jean Rhys are a selection of recognisable names, but there are hundreds more whose contributions to literature have been forgotten. A list of Bloomsbury poets would be likewise lengthy. Despite the proliferation of commemorative plaques that mark the residencies of literary figures in the area, Bloomsbury's absolute centrality to the production of imaginative writing is still underappreciated, the dominance of the Bloomsbury Group within the popular cultural imagination seeming to have occluded to a certain extent the area's much more general historical association with the practice of writing. Despite this, it is telling – though not at all surprising – that there are substantially more blue plaques for Bloomsbury writers than for Bloomsbury lawyers. Whether or not novelists or poets are really 'the hierophants of an unapprehended inspiration', the memory of dead literary men and women is kept alive today much more assiduously, and lovingly, than those of the lawyers that lived and died alongside them in Bloomsbury's streets and squares.

For Thomas Burke, Bloomsbury's association with imaginative writing had an intense, palpable, effect on the locality, lending it an unusual air of freedom: 'One of the charms of Bloomsbury is that, in a reasonable way, you can do "that there" and quite a lot of other things. In its student atmosphere you are freer than in some other parts of London . . . For Bloomsbury is mainly literature and art, which are the madness of humans engaged in reproducing the sanity of the gods.'[12]

For some writers, such as George Gissing, this way of seeing Bloomsbury as somehow more autonomous and free than other parts of London was just a vain nostalgic illusion. In his *New Grub Street* (1891), literary Bloomsbury is represented as the 'valley of the shadow of books', the literary environs of the British Museum being just as rule-bound and market-driven as Fleet Street or the City. In one particularly gloomy passage Marian Yule, a hack-writer, is sitting gloomily in the British Museum's reading room when she realises that literary production in modernity is more like machine labour than the prophecy Shelley sees as literature's natural function:

> It was ignoble to sit here and support the paltry pretence of intellectual dignity. A few days ago her startled eye had caught an advertisement in the newspaper, headed 'Literary Machine'; had it then been invented at last, some automaton to supply the place of such poor creatures as herself to turn out books and articles? Alas! the machine was only one for holding volumes conveniently, that the work of literary manufacture might be physically lightened. But surely before long some Edison would make the true automaton; the problem must be comparatively such a simple one. Only to throw in a given number of old books, and have them reduced, blended, modernised into a single one for to-day's consumption.
>
> The fog grew thicker; she looked up at the windows beneath the dome and saw that they were a dusky yellow. Then her eye discerned an official walking along the upper gallery, and in pursuance of her grotesque humour, her mocking misery, she likened him to a black, lost soul, doomed to wander in an eternity of vain research along endless shelves. Or again, the readers who sat here at these radiating lines of desks, what were they but hapless flies caught in a huge web, its nucleus the great circle of the Catalogue? Darker, darker. From the towering wall of volumes seemed to emanate visible motes, intensifying the obscurity; in a moment the book-lined circumference of the room would be but a featureless prison-limit.

But then flashed forth the sputtering whiteness of the electric light, and its ceaseless hum was henceforth a new source of headache. It reminded her how little work she had done to-day; she must, she must force herself to think of the task in hand. A machine has no business to refuse its duty. But the pages were blue and green and yellow before her eyes; the uncertainty of the light was intolerable. Right or wrong she would go home, and hide herself, and let her heart unburden itself of tears.[13]

Far from being free to dream up the future, Marion feels all too severely the deterministic weight of present duties.

To what extent writers are free to shape the world through their words or hemmed in by the 'prison-limit' of material reality is a problem that has often been posed, though never effectively solved, in Bloomsbury. A poem by Louis MacNeice, written ominously in 1939, turns again to the British Museum to think about the relationship of writing to power. Resisting the absolute pessimism of Gissing's *New Grub Street*, MacNeice's 'The British Museum Reading Room' leaves the problem in the balance somewhat:

> Under the hive-like dome the stooping haunted readers
> Go up and down the alleys, tap the cells of knowledge –
> Honey and wax, the accumulation of years . . .
> Some on commission, some for the love of learning,
> Some because they have nothing better to do
> Or because they hope these walls of books will deaden
> The drumming of the demon in their ears.
>
> Cranks, hacks, poverty-stricken scholars,
> In prince-nez, period hats or romantic beards
> And cherishing their hobby or their doom,
> Some are too much alive and some are asleep
> Hanging like bats in a world of inverted values,
> Folded up in themselves in a world which is safe and silent:
> This is the British Museum Reading Room.

'Reading-Room, British Museum,' in Thomas Greenwood, *Free Public Libraries, Their Organisation, Uses and Management*. London 1886.

Out on the steps in the sun the pigeons are courting,
Puffing their ruffs and sweeping their tails or taking
A sun-bath at their ease
And under the totem poles – the ancient terror –
Between the enormous fluted ionic columns
There seeps from heavily jowled or hawk-like foreign faces
The guttural sorrow of the refugees.[14]

The 'world of inverted values' that the dreaming writers witness – hanging as they are like bats, upside down – might be a 'safe' and irrelevant illusion, cordoned off from the violent world of bad legislation that is driving refugees into the bosom of this 'hive-like dome'. Alternatively, the eccentric literary vision engendered within this oddball space might signal real 'hope', a word the poem cannot help but utter, despite its misgivings about the mixed motivations and apparent dead ends of all the reading and writing that goes on there.

Hanging like those bats, undecided, the poem leaves us with an ambivalent sense of the *difference* literary language makes – a difference that is surely Bloomsbury's special gift and its lasting secret.

Notes

Preface

1. Walford 1878, vol. 4, p. 480.
2. Surtees 1903, pp. 73–74.
3. Collins 1883, vol. 1, pp. 16–17.

1. Budding

1. Levy 1889, p. 17.
2. Cowper 1934, p. 661.
3. Ryskamp 1959, p. 120.
4. Dickens 2003, p. 319.
5. Porter and Porter 1828, vol. 3
6. Longstaffe-Gowan 2012, p. 177.
7. Hill 1883, p. 2.
8. Dickens and Morley 1852, pp. 45–48.
9. Mew 2008, pp. 27–28.

2. Aspiring

1. Ashton 2012. Chapter 1 is devoted to the topic and the phrase.
2. Hardy 1976, 'The Levelled Graveyard' [1882], pp. 157–58.
3. Quoted from 'About Senate House', http://www.london. ac.uk/aboutsenatehouse. html.
4. Anon (*Morning Chronicle*) 1826, p. 3.
5. Anon (*Gentleman's Magazine*) 1828, pp. 293–96.
6. Du Maurier 1897, p. 162.
7. Anon (*Leisure Hour*) 1857, pp. 519–22.
8. Anand 1981, p. 5.
9. Lucas 1906, pp. 221–23.
10. Kendall 2008, p. 183.
11. Ackroyd 1993, p. 185.

3. Connecting

1. Lucas 1906, p. 221.
2. Ibid., p. 223.
3. James 2003, p. 98.
4. Ibid., p. 53.
5. Rhys 1981, p. 99.
6. Quoted in Ahmed 2012, p. 70.
7. Hay 1922, p. 58.
8. Ibid., p. 67.

9. Ibid., p. 83.
10. Oliphant 1894, p. 3.
11. Ibid., pp. 34–35.
12. Millais 1899, p. 49.
13. Ibid., p. 51.
14. Woolf 2002, p. 57.

4. Railing

1. http://www.britishpathe.com/
   video/bloomsbury-issue-
   title-is-out-and-about/query/
   Square.
2. Orwell 1970a, p. 234.
3. Anon (*Preston Guardian*)
   1874, p. 2.
4. Anon (*Graphic*) 1874, p. 222.
5. Morris 1993, p. 85.
6. James 2003, p. 97.
7. Ibid., p. 44.
8. Anand 1981, p. 24.
9. Hobhouse 1900, p. 483.
10. Ford 1895, pp. 10–11.
11. W. H. Kendall, open letter to
    Mary Allen of the Women's
    Social and Political Union,
    The Times, 14 June 1913.
12. 'The Funeral of Miss
    Davison', *The Times*, 16
    June 1913.

5. Timing

1. Dickens 1854, 'The Boarding
   House: II' [1834], p. 180.
2. Richardson 1919, pp. 54–56.
3. Stevenson and Stevenson
   1885, p. 185.

4. Ibid., p. 189.
5. Burke 1929, p. 19.
6. Burke 1939, p. 165.
7. James 2003, pp. 51–52.
8. Pritchett 1986, pp. 117–18.
9. Lucas 1906, p. 224.
10. Anon (*Fun*) 1871, p. 159.
11. Keats 1988, pp. 99–100.
12. Hardy 1976, 'In the British
    Museum'[1914], pp. 381–82.
13. Hardy 1997, p. 177.
14. Nesbit 1907, pp. 187–92.
15. Carter 2006, p. 346.

6. Wording

1. Roget 1852, Preface.
2. Quoted in Kendall 2008, p. 3.
3. Ibid., p. 262.
4. Orwell 1970b, p. 166.
5. Letter from T. S. Eliot
   to Geoffrey Faber,
   April 1936, http://www.
   booktrade.info/index.php/
   showarticle/22968.
6. Jeaffreson 1867, p. 37.
7. Quoted in Kendall 2008,
   pp. 197–98.
8. Linebaugh 2003, p. 357.
9. Dickens 2003, pp. 551–52.
10. Dickens 1998, p. 677.
11. Shelley 1998, pp. 944–56.
12. Burke 1939, p. 165.
13. Gissing 2016, pp. 95–96.
14. MacNeice 1966, 'The
    British Museum Reading
    Room' [1939], p. 160.

Further Reading

Ackroyd 1993: Peter Ackroyd, *Hawksmoor* [1985], Penguin 1993.

Ahmed 2012: Rehana Ahmed, 'Networks of Resistance: Krishna Menon and Working-Class South Asians in Inter-War Britain', in Rehana Ahmed and Sumita Mukherjee (ed.), *South Asian Resistances in Britain, 1858–1947*, Continuum 2012.

Anand 1981: Mulk Raj Anand, *Conversations in Bloomsbury*, Wildwood House 1981.

Anon (*Fun*) 1871: 'The Groves of Bloomsbury', *Fun*, 22 April 1871.

Anon (*Gentleman's Magazine*) 1828: 'The London University', *Gentleman's Magazine and Historical Chronicle*, October 1828.

Anon (*Graphic*) 1874: 'Topics of the Week', *Graphic*, 5 September 1874, no. 249.

Anon (*Leisure Hour*) 1857: 'New Reading-Room at the British Museum', *Leisure Hour: A Family Journal of Instruction and Recreation*, vol. 294, 13 August 1857.

Anon (*Morning Chronicle*) 1826: 'Increase of London, from the Rage of Building', *Morning Chronicle*, 25 October 1826.

Anon (*Preston Guardian*) 1874: 'Metropolitan Gossip', *Preston Guardian etc.*, 19 December 1874, no. 3232.

Ashton 2012: Rosemary Ashton, *Victorian Bloomsbury*, Yale University Press 2012.

Barnett 2008: Richard Barnett, *Anatomy of the City: A Guide to Medical London*, Wellcome Trust 2008.

Bernstein 2013: Susan David Bernstein, *Roomscape: Women Writers at the British Museum from George Eliot to Virginia Woolf*, Edinburgh University Press 2013.

Besant and Mitton 1903: Walter Besant and G. E. Mitton, *The Fascination of London: Holborn and Bloomsbury*, Adam & Charles Black 1903.

Black 2006: Nick Black, *Walking London's Medical History*, Royal Society of Medicine Press 2006.

Blair 2004: Sara Blair, 'Local Modernity, Global Modernism: Bloomsbury and the Places of the Literary', *ELH*, vol. 71, no. 3, 2004, pp. 813–38.

Boehm 2009: Katharina Boehm, '"A Place for More than the Healing of Bodily Sickness": Charles Dickens, the Social Mission of Nineteenth-Century Pediatrics, and the Great Ormond Street Hospital for Sick Children,' *Victorian Review*, vol. 35, no. 1, 2009, pp. 153–74.

Burke 1929: Thomas Burke, *The Bloomsbury Wonder*, The Mandrake Press 1929.

Burke 1939: Thomas Burke, *Living in Bloomsbury*, G. Allen & Unwin 1939.

Carter 2006: Angela Carter, *Nights at the Circus* [1984], Vintage 2006.

Collins 1883: Wilkie Collins, *Heart and Science: A Story of the Present Time*, Chatto & Windus 1883, 3 vols.

Cowper 1934: William Cowper, 'To my dearest cousin on her removal of us from Silver End, to Weston', H. S. Milford (ed.), *The Poetical Works of William Cowper*, 4th ed., Oxford University Press 1934.

Dennis 2009: Richard Dennis, 'The Place of Bloomsbury in the Novels of George Gissing', *Opticon 1826*, no. 7, 2009.

Dickens 1854: Charles Dickens, *Sketches by Boz*, Chapman & Hall 1854.

Dickens 1998: Charles Dickens, *Bleak House* [1853], Oxford University Press 1998.

Dickens 2003: Charles Dickens, *Barnaby Rudge* [1841], Penguin 2003.

Dickens and Morley 1852: Charles Dickens and Henry Morley, 'Drooping Buds', *Household Words*, vol. V, no. 106, 3 April 1852.

Du Maurier 1897: George Du Maurier, *The Martian*, Harper & Brothers 1897.

Ford 1895: Isabella Ford, *On the Threshold*, Edward Arnold 1895.

Gissing 2016: George Gissing, *New Grub Street* [1891],

Oxford University Press 2016.

Hardy 1976: James Gibson (ed.), *The Complete Poems of Thomas Hardy*, Macmillan 1976.

Hardy 1997: Thomas Hardy, *The Hand of Ethelberta* [1876], Penguin 1997.

Hay 1922: Ian Hay, *Tilly of Bloomsbury: A Comedy in Three Acts* [1919], Samuel French Ltd 1922.

Hill 1883: Octavia Hill, letter to the editor, 'London Gardens for the Poor', *Standard* (London), 11 July 1883.

Hoberman 2002: Ruth Hoberman, 'Women in the British Museum Reading Room during the Late-Nineteenth and Early-Twentieth Centuries: From Quasi- to Counterpublic', *Feminist Studies*, vol. 28, no. 3, 2002, pp. 489–512.

Hobhouse 1990: Emily Hobhouse, 'Women Workers: How they Live, How they Wish to Live', *Nineteenth Century: A Monthly Review*, vol. 47, no. 277, March 1900.

James 2003: C. L. R. James, *Letters from London*, Signal Books 2003.

Jeaffreson 1867: John Cordy Jeaffreson, *A Book about Lawyers*, G. W. Carleton & Co. 1867.

Keats 1988: John Keats, 'On Seeing the Elgin Marbles' [1817], in John Barnard (ed.), *John Keats: The Complete Poems*, Penguin 1988.

Kendall 2008: Joshua C. Kendall, *The Man Who Made Lists: Love, Death, Madness, and the Creation of Roget's Thesaurus*, G. P. Putnam's Sons 2008.

Kosky 1989: Jules Kosky, *Mutual Friends: Charles Dickens and Great Ormond Street Children's Hospital*, Weidenfeld & Nicolson 1989.

Levy 1889: Amy Levy, *A London Plane-Tree and Other Verse*, T. Fisher Unwin 1889.

Linebaugh 2003: Peter Linebaugh, *The London Hanged: Crime and Civil Society in the Eighteenth Century*, Verso 2003.

Livesey 2007: Ruth Livesey, 'Socialism in Bloomsbury: Virginia Woolf and the Political Aesthetics of the 1880s', *The Yearbook of English Studies*, vol. 37, no. 1, 2007, pp. 126–44.

Longstaffe-Gowan 2012: Todd Longstaffe-Gowan, *The London Square: Gardens in the Midst of Town*, Yale University Press 2012.

Lucas 1906: E. V. Lucas, *A Wanderer in London*, Methuen & Co. 1906.

MacNeice 1966: E. R. Dodds (ed.), *The Collected Poems of Louis MacNeice*, Faber & Faber Ltd 1966.

Mew 2008: Charlotte Mew, 'The Trees are Down' [1920], from *Selected Poems*, Carcanet 2008.

Millais 1899: John Guille Millais, *The Life and Letters of Sir John Everett Millais, President of the Royal Academy*, Methuen 1899, vol. 1.

Morris 1993: William Morris, *News from Nowhere and Other Writings*, Penguin 1993.

Murray 2014: Nicholas Murray, *Bloomsbury and the Poets*, Rack Press Editions 2014.

Nesbit 1907: Edith Nesbit, *The Story of the Amulet* [1906], E. P. Dutton & Co. 1907.

Oliphant 1894: Margaret Oliphant, *A House in Bloomsbury*, Hutchinson & Co. 1894.

Olsen 1982: Donald Olsen, *Town Planning in London: The Eighteenth and Nineteenth Centuries*, revised ed, Yale University Press 1982.

Orwell 1970a: George Orwell, 'As I Please' [*Tribune*, 4 August 1944], in *The Collected Essays, Journalism and Letters of George Orwell Vol. 3: As I Please, 1943–1945*, Penguin 1970.

Orwell 1970b: George Orwell, 'Politics and the English Language', in *The Collected Essays, Journalism and Letters of George Orwell, Vol. 4: In Front of Your Nose, 1945–1950*, Penguin 1970.

Pollak Williamson 2015: Catalina Pollak Williamson, *Outsider: Public Art and the Politics of the English Garden Square*, Common Editions 2015.

Porter and Porter 1828: Jane Porter and Anne Porter, *Coming Out; and The Field of Forty Footsteps*, Longmans 1828, 3 vols.

Pritchett 1986: V. S. Pritchett, *London Perceived*, Hogarth 1986.

Richardson 1919: Dorothy Richardson, *Interim*,

Duckworth 1919.

Rhys 1981: Jean Rhys, *Smile Please: An Unfinished Autobiography*, Penguin 1981.

Roget 1852: Peter Mark Roget, *Thesaurus of English Words and Phrases*, Longmans 1852.

Ryskamp 1959: Charles Ryskamp, *William Cowper of the Inner Temple Esquire: A Study of His Life and Works to the Year 1768*, Cambridge University Press 1959.

Shelley 1998: Percy Shelley, 'A Defence of Poetry' [1821, 1840], in Duncan Wu (ed.), *Romanticism: An Anthology*, Blackwell Publishers 1998.

Snaith 2014: Anna Snaith, *Modernist Voyages: Colonial Women Writers in London, 1890–1945*, Cambridge University Press 2014.

Stevenson and Stevenson 1885: Robert Louis Stevenson and Fanny Van de Grift Stevenson, *More Arabian Nights: The Dynamiter*, Longmans, Green & Co. 1885.

Surtees 1903: R. W. Surtees, *Handley Cross* [1843], D. Appleton & Company 1903.

Tambling 2009: Jeremy Tambling, *Going Astray: Dickens and London*, Pearson Education Ltd 2009.

Tames 1993: Richard Tames, *Bloomsbury Past: A Visual History*, Historical Publications 1993.

Vadillo 2005: Ana Parejo Vadillo, *Women Poets and Urban Aestheticism: Passengers of Modernity*, Palgrave Macmillan 2005.

Walford 1878: Edward Walford. *Old and New London: A Narrative of its History, its People, and its Places* (6 vols), Cassell 1878, vol. 4.

White 2008: Jerry White, *London in the Nineteenth Century: 'A Human Awful Wonder of God'*, Vintage 2008.

Woolf 2002: Virginia Woolf, *Moments of Being: Autobiographical Writings* [1976], Pimlico 2002.

Picture Credits

Acknowledgements

Writers usually find Acknowledgements an absorbing genre to read, in part because they know quite how hard they can be to write; fairly, honestly, kindly, wisely. The process of selection is a tough tightrope walk, unless one goes for the safe options – those polar opposites of narcissistic excess or laconic opacity. This one intends to tread a *via media*, picking out a few specific names but leaving others every bit as important to me scrawled in invisible ink over so many of this book's pages.

Thanks are due to my school teachers at DHSB, Plymouth, especially from the English department, who prompted me to read grown-up books that helped me grow up, and also to appreciate how reading might be a political act; from the History department, who led me to understand that engaging with the past might be one of the ways in which we imagine and shape the future; and from the Music department, who encouraged me to seek full immersion in the pleasures and pains of the present, and who bolstered my self-esteem at a period in my life when it was otherwise at a low ebb. To John Bowden, who introduced me at an early age to Stravinsky and, through that, helped me learn that otherness was a relative rather than an essential property, and that initially difficult objects – and people – were worth actively pursuing. To Dick Bell, for that argument we had at Upcott back in my mid-teens, in which he introduced me to the idea that universities, being full of communists, might be dangerous to young minds, thus sparking a desire to end up teaching in one.

To all my teachers and friends from Oxford, and in particular Robert Douglas-Fairhurst, for the Svengali-like conjuring tricks he performed in undergraduate tutorials to convince us all to aspire to be more attentive readers and better writers; to Mina Gorji, for affirming that an interest in style need not be incompatible with radical class politics; and to Rob Gilbert, who was a model of generous support when we all needed that. To all my teachers, colleagues and friends from UCL's English department, especially my primary doctoral supervisor Rosemary Ashton, who taught me to appreciate London not only as a stimulant to thought but also for its historical particularity; and to Greg Dart, for reminding me that my new enthusiasm for facts didn't require a complete excision of a previous attraction to theory. To colleagues in the Geography department there too, for flattering me on occasion by telling me they sometimes forgot I wasn't one of their tribe. To colleagues at UCL's Centre for Languages and International Education, for sustaining a supportive environment to research and teach in for my first job. To Markman Ellis and Paul Hamilton, of QMUL's School of English and Drama, who took a punt on me for my second job and have both been relentlessly kind ever since. Likewise to all my other colleagues there, whose collective wisdom, tolerance and strength has often been a tonic, and from whom I have learnt a great deal, already, after only three years with them.

To Jenny Bourne Taylor and Matthew Beaumont for being generous and stringent in their examination of my doctoral thesis, out of which emerged my continuing intellectual engagement with the problem of Bloomsbury. To the place itself, and all of the beginnings, aspirations, connections, obstacles, moments, dreams and deadlines I've met (with) there.

To those who, very kindly, read drafts of parts of this text and, in particular, to Tom Dillon, John Dunn, Matthew J. Holman, Ceri Owen and Christopher Webb.

To the team at British Library publishing, especially Rob Davies, Miranda Harrison and Sally Nicholls, who have been supportive, patient and diligent in their work to help me get this book into shape. Also to the staff in general at the British Library, where I wrote pretty much every single one of its sentences.

To my family for having early nurtured in me a hunch that commitments to truth, freedom and love need not be mutually incompatible, and my friends, of all sorts and conditions, for having refreshed and sustained this hunch in years since.

Index

References in *italic* indicate pages on which illustrations appear